JESUS and ETERNITY

JESUS and ETERNITY

JESUS and ETERNITY

PEACE for FEAR

PEACE for FEAR

PEACE for FEAR

'A *must-read for our difficult days*' — Michael A.G. Haykin

Michael Austin

DayOne

© Day One Publications 2022

ISBN 978-1-84625-709-4

British Library Cataloguing in Publication Data available

Day One Publications
Ryelands Road, Leominster, HR6 8NZ, England
Tel 01568 613 740
North America Toll Free 888 329 6630
email sales@dayone.co.uk
web www.dayone.co.uk

The image on the cover is used under licence from Shutterstock.com

Printed by 4edge Limited

Commendations

This helpful evangelistic book is challenging yet winsome. Modern psychology cannot answer life's aching need. And all the self-help schemes, reasoning, and philosophy of men are powerless to deliver from eternal judgement. Love warns, and the author wonderfully presents Christ as the only Saviour for eternity.

Philip Bell
CEO of Creation Ministries International
(UK/Europe)

We are living in trying times: the political scene, both domestic and international, rent by anger, vitriol, the pandemic and war and the frenetic pace of change, are producing deep-seated despair and fear. This small book reminds us that the Scriptures address this dread and terror directly, with the offer of the love of Christ who has conquered both death and hell. A must-read for our difficult days.

Michael A. G. Haykin
Chair and Professor of Church History,
The Southern Baptist Theological Seminary, USA

The fear of death and of eternity is much more common than you might think. We have made it a taboo subject. We deal with it by denial, but even so it is the hidden cause of a great deal of ill-health and distress. I am grateful for this concise yet thorough little book by Michael Austin that not only exposes the roots of our fears but also points to the only possible answer.

Dr Stephen McAuley MB BCh BAO
Doctor, Counsellor and now pastor of
Killicomaine Evangelical Church

Commendations

In this book Michael Austin deals clearly with two great biblical realities—Jesus, God's beloved Son, and the glory of eternity. He shows that through Jesus we can find peace with God now. Jesus delivers us from all our fears and promises the joy of being with God in heaven for ever.

Peter Milsom
Chairman of the Associating Evangelical Churches of Wales

I am pleased to commend this book which gives particular focus on the fears we might all experience at the prospect of death and uncertainties about our infinite existence. The book takes us through how and why Jesus is the answer to our fears and the object of our comfort and hope.

Graham Nicholls
Director of Affinity

This comprehensive book is a vital help. It covers an issue which is found in every society and every heart. A book to change and convince an atheist, strengthen and equip a struggling or troubled believer, it powerfully shows us how Jesus Christ is the only answer to the fears that dominate us.

Pastor Mark Stocker
Southampton

Acknowledgements

To Daphne, my wife, a special word of loving appreciation for her patience and prayer, without which this little book would not have seen the light of day.

Warm thanks to Professor Michael Haykin, Dr Stephen McAuley, Peter Milsom, and Graham Nicolls, who, despite heavy work commitments, kindly offered to read the manuscript and offer commendations.

Particular thanks are due to Philip Bell and Mark Stocker who, beyond their commendations, also generously shared detailed and very helpful suggestions.

Sincere thanks also to Mark Roberts, Managing Director of Day One Publications, who was pleased to accept this new book, and assign Keith Weber to the project. I am very grateful to him for his astute editing and his exceptional cover design.

Contents

The challenge of ETERNITY

Fear is possibly the strongest human emotion, and it is widespread. Some fears warn of danger, like when we smell smoke and hear crackling roof timbers. Others may be symptoms of insecurity or the result of many other problems.

As to the fear of eternity, I have found that many people, including atheists, are troubled by the thought. But, quite apart from the many millions who have faced eternity during the COVID epidemic, never have so many people been alive at the same time as there are today.

The fact is: we all face ETERNITY. Facing that challenge, this book looks at Jesus and his answer for fear.

I approach this subject with the conviction that Jesus is the final answer for the deepest problems of our humanity. Faith in him is nothing like blind trust or a leap in the dark, but rather the most reasonable step of personal trust.

Jesus spoke to this fearful world of troubled hearts and minds—*do not be anxious about your life...!* (Matthew 6:25).[1] He knows the root cause of anxious minds, and the solution.

Whether you profess Christian belief, have a religious upbringing, or have secular, atheistic, or meditation-based beliefs—the challenge of ETERNITY is one you need to face.

---

1 All Bible quotes are in *italic* type followed by the reference, chapter and verse, in brackets, as this example.

1. Why Jesus?

Why Jesus in the first place? One answer is, because that is his place. After his mission in this world, God exalted Jesus *far above all rule and authority and power and dominion, and above every name that is named* (Ephesians 1:21). He is supreme. What has that got to do with eternity?

Everything. Speaking of himself, Jesus said, whoever *believes in the Son has eternal life* (John 3:36).

His claim made that doubly clear: *I am the resurrection and the life. Whoever believes in me, though he die, yet shall he live, and everyone who lives and believes in me shall never die* (John 11:25–26). Jesus is the source of eternal life, and *Jesus Christ is Lord* (Philippians 2:11).

He is the answer

He has the answers about eternity and for the fear of it. These are large claims. Does Jesus' life back them up? His life is on public record in the four Gospels for all to review.

> His life is on public record in the four Gospels for all to review

Jesus came to public attention with a striking challenge of good news: *The time is fulfilled, and the kingdom of God is at hand; repent and believe in the gospel* (Mark 1:15).

He was the unique King, the Messiah, and the Prince of Peace, who had come on a mission in which he, *the good shepherd lays down his life for the sheep* (John 10:11). He also foretold that his good news *will be proclaimed throughout the whole world* (Matthew 24:14).

Jesus' birth was announced from heaven. Yet, he worked as a carpenter, called fishermen as his first followers, but spoke with such authority that at times the crowds were enthralled at the God of great compassion and power, even if they did not recognise that he had come down to them in his own Son.

Chapter 1

He was the answer to the age-old promise of the prophets, as he told his followers: *But blessed are your eyes, for they see, and your ears, for they hear. For truly, I say to you, many prophets and righteous people longed to see what you see, and did not see it, and to hear what you hear, and did not hear it* (Matthew 13:16–17).

But, Jesus was no ordinary King: he welcomed social and moral outcasts, forgave their sins, opened the eyes of the blind, cleansed lepers and raised the dead. These events and many others were signs that confirmed Jesus' claim to be the Son of God, which were well-documented by eyewitness reports given in the Gospels.

In spite of all the learning of the religious leaders of Jesus' day, they were blind to one vital truth. They did not know that their hostile jealousy of Jesus, stirred by his popularity, by his signs, and his scathing denunciation of their hypocrisy, would fulfil their own Scriptures to the letter *by condemning him* (Acts 13:27).

He is the Lord

Those leaders did not recognise even their own heaven-sent Messiah. In the sequel, despite Jesus' violent death, he already knew this was central to why God had sent him into the world. He had repeatedly said that he would *be killed, and after three days rise again* (Mark 8:31). Indeed, he was killed, *but God raised him from the dead* (Acts 13:30).

Remarkably, the evidence for Jesus' resurrection still stands as credible and compelling. The eyewitness accounts of the disciples' fears, the empty tomb and Jesus' appearances after his resurrection remain fully convincing. On the basis of *many proofs* (Acts 1:3), we face him, for *Jesus Christ is the same yesterday, today and forever* (Hebrews 13:8).

> The evidence for Jesus' resurrection still stands as credible and compelling

Why Jesus? He existed before time began. Addressing God his Father, Jesus said, *you loved me before the foundation of the world* (John 17:24). He then gave himself into death and proved his power over it. On top of that he said he had *all authority in heaven and on earth* (Matthew 28:18).

Jesus is one of us, yet different. His message of eternal hope and peace is as up-to date as ever. After he had stilled a storm with convincing authority over nature, he said to his awestruck followers in their little boat, *Why are you so afraid? Have you still no faith?* (Mark 4:40).

Jesus Christ is the one in whom *all the fullness of God was pleased to dwell* (Colossians 1:19). No situation is beyond him—he is the Lord of the cosmos, of heart and mind. He is the Lord of eternity.

'Why Jesus?' He, like no one else, understands us, our failures, anxieties and our fears—even fear of him. Later, you'll see more of the reasons why.

2. Fear of eternity

When I discovered that people were suffering from 'eternity phobia', what surprised me most was how these fears were not unusual—and they were being shared openly.

A typical edited post reads: 'At times I get this obsessive thought that I am going to exist forever and ever, and it is such a paralysing fear. My anxiety attacks about ETERNITY are horrible! Now I know that other people have this same awful phobia, but I still don't know if there is a remedy or how to deal with it.' Some posts are from people who say they are Christians; some mention God, and some are from teenagers.

> 'At times I get this obsessive thought that I am going to exist forever and ever, and it is such a paralysing fear'

Fear is common

Of course, there is often relief gained by writing about our fears and discovering others have similar problems, and then finding that fear is common and often the result of anxious worry.

We all know anxiety can have very different causes. Some are quite mild, but types of severe anxiety may trigger uncontrollable or deep-seated fears, perhaps by particular associations. These tend to become repetitive and sufficiently troubling to be called a 'phobia', and at times linked to the fairly common experience of a panic attack.

In general, what we call 'fear' is a response to a particular event or stimulus. A release from the adrenal glands triggers our sense of alarm and readiness to 'fight-or-flight' that causes heart-beat and breathing-rate to increase and muscles to be energised for action.

Fear-stirring events are those like being crushed by a dense crowd, when people begin to panic, or particular thoughts like eternity that trigger a sense of alarm. One stimulus is an external event, which you see was a good reason for feeling very alarmed. But the other, inner response to those fear-creating thoughts of an unknown eternity seems just as real. But oh, if only those fears weren't so horrible!

Secular views

Today, secular humanism believes reason can answer life's problems. This sort of confidence has no time for religious beliefs. In particular, based on the assumption that secular beliefs, including atheism, are marks of superior intellectual and scientific progress, it rejects the claims of Christianity.

Here we draw a line, because many deep-seated problems have roots that are either not understood or rejected by those with humanistic or secular world views. Certainly, secular counselling may help to desensitise agoraphobia—the fear of public or open spaces—and other well-known fears. Some fears may stem from experiences like a childhood attendance at a funeral, others like social anxiety or insecurity may point to social stress and awkward difficulties.

Here, the distinction of a professional psychologist is worth noting: 'The current plethora of psychotherapeutic approaches can offer temporary relief from emotional pain, but they can never meet the deepest needs of the human heart.'[2]

> 'The current plethora of psychotherapeutic approaches ... can never meet the deepest needs of the human heart'

Beneath the emotional pain, God has revealed a far greater problem—you won't like it, but *all have sinned* (Romans 3:23). Instead of obeying him, we have done the opposite, and as a result, have true moral guilt before God. But trying to conceal a fear of judgement by secular counselling only evades the truth and never brings peace with God.

Long before the rise of secular psychology, people faced fears, cholera epidemics, broken relationships, wars, death, disease, and obsessive thoughts. Many were fearful, introspective or highly strung and faced

---

2 Chris Thurman, Ph.D., *Totally Sufficient—The Bible & Christian Counselling* (Christian Focus, Ross-shire, Great Britain), 2004, p. 90.

great difficulties. You are not alone. But, beneath all the fear and trouble is the deeper issue of how to get right with God.

Positive help

Many of these people, especially after the sixteenth century rediscovery of the gospel, had a clear personal trust in Christ. They had heard the good news of God's undeserved favour—his grace—and had trusted in Jesus Christ for the forgiveness of their sins.

That was a time when the Bible had become more available in the West, and when people with difficulties often turned to it for help. People bereaved or suffering personal anxieties often found assurance and peace from the Psalms. Many of them express the heart cry of faith; for instance, *I sought the LORD, and he answered me and delivered me from all my fears* (Psalm 34:4). Those few words have helped many.

In the biblical Christian churches that followed the Reformation in the sixteenth century, there was a pastoral emphasis to help those troubled by a guilty conscience, or worrying trials and fears. These pastors had moved far from the practice of private confessions, as they carefully shared the detailed teaching of the word of God.

By this practice many, who were not able to own a Bible, found encouragement and fresh hope. They came to see that God's word was wonderfully sufficient and included words that suited their own mind and conscience, as well as their circumstances.

What do we face today? Many assume that a mental health professional has high up-to-date competence compared with a pastor who only has his Bible-based beliefs. Just as we would expect, a secular specialist may offer a troubled and anxious person relief, either by counselling, referral to a support group, or by medication.

Final authority

However, only biblical Christianity gives a complete answer to our human condition. This is why I explain the flawed thinking of atheistic and secular

God's self-credible word ... does not need to be authenticated or approved by an independent authority

belief and defend the sufficiency of the Bible's teaching to offer help for our fears.

This view accepts the claims of Scripture to be God's self-credible word that does not need to be authenticated or approved by an independent authority. This is where we see what God's word teaches about our creation in the image of God, and the awful ravages of the historic Genesis fall, in which we all now share.

We share this in several ways, as sinners under God's judgement, which includes our genetic or physical and social inheritance. In the time that has elapsed from the creation of our first parents up to the present, we are all affected variously by gradual genetic loss, by small mutations, and by inheriting particular difficulties, physical, social, or psychological, over which we had no choice.

We share much in common, but at times a strange, obsessive unease comes to many about what lies after death and whether that will bring a never-ending consciousness. They face the fear of eternity. Some are so awed by their insignificance or meaninglessness in so vast a cosmos that they become alarmed by the unbearable thought that time for them will never end.

This can leave people feeling tense and in need to find ways to relax their stressed minds.

At times a strange, obsessive unease comes to many about what lies after death and whether that will bring a never-ending consciousness

Reduced intensity

Our own sense of unique individuality can be a powerful force, driving fears into the depths of solitary confinement, where they may become uncontrollable tyrants. Finding that one is not alone and that these difficult subjects can be talked about with a sympathetic listener may be a very practical way to scale down the high intensity of a phobia or of any situation that provokes fear.

Even for Christians who have a clear assurance of heaven—and assurance is a vital subject that we shall discuss later—the fear-filled thoughts of eternity or infinity may still grip our minds.

Some who may be troubled by a morbid, obsessive fascination with their fears will appreciate a positive way forward.

Introspective people seem more aware of how their deep thoughts affect their self-awareness and how these cause their peace, on the one hand, or their doubts and fears, on the other. Many are also highly strung and troubled by their storms of emotion.

What has brought this fear of eternity into public prominence is the rise of social media platforms, coupled with a greater social acceptance of talking about subjects that were once taboo.

Combine this with the rise of popular psychology, mental health professionals, and various spirituality and meditation practitioners, who offer hope, peace of mind, and help for stress, panic attacks, addictive behaviours and poor relationships (for a start), and we have the present familiar situation.

Conditioning

Many who suffer from fears like that of flying, of high-rise buildings, or open spaces, may gradually be desensitised to those situations and find confidence with the help of a professional specialist.

Our mind carries the strong memories of childhood—which become part of our adult thought-life, and cannot just be shrugged off however hard we try.

Thoughts of eternity that focus on its never-endingness are potent. There is no doubt that for sufferers this is a daunting and powerful subject. Sometimes, just to see a larger context in which to place fears that seem to defy understanding can help to shrink them.

> Thoughts of eternity that focus on its never-endingness are potent

Jesus is Lord

With all these thoughts, we will see that Jesus' teaching is not aimed at merely bringing psychological relief to our anxious fears or our difficult circumstances. His teaching is certainly very practical, but, first and foremost, he calls people to come to him and find him as the one who gives them peace with God.

So this book is not a self-help manual for personal fears. Whatever insights you gain along the way, the big challenge is eternity and to find peace with God.

Jesus is first—he is Lord and central in the good news of God's offer to rescue us from an eternal loss and freely give an eternal relationship with him.

> Jesus is first—he is Lord and central in the good news of God's offer to rescue us from an eternal loss and freely give an eternal relationship with him

Consider this as the challenge of a new way forward and how Jesus is relevant to your life. Yes, you may well have a question about that. If the Bible is so old, how can it help me today?

3. Is the Bible sufficient?

If the Bible is so old, is the Christian approach to helping those with fears one which integrates insights from secular counselling models, or does it rely wholly on the Bible? The sufficiency of Scripture with Jesus at the centre is so vital that we devote this chapter to explain it.

Modern medical practice may use medication to treat various diseases of the brain, but this is not in conflict with our confidence in the sufficiency of the Bible. The Bible never claims to be a medical text for such conditions or, for instance, such physical problems as bone fractures, detached retinas, diabetes, or organ transplants.

However, many serious anxieties, which have been labelled 'disorders' or an 'illness' by secular thought, are problems for which biblical counselling is fully sufficient; a view endorsed by many medical professionals.[3] The Bible stands on its own claims to be God's inspired word, a wholly sufficient guide to find salvation in Christ and for the whole of life. For a start, Jesus endorsed the Old Testament Scriptures and confirmed that *it is they that bear witness about me* (John 5:39).

Jesus is central

He never hesitated to place himself at the centre of God's written revelation. Time and again Jesus quoted the Scriptures and always upheld their divine authority. In his time of temptation by the devil, Jesus resisted every time, first by saying *it is written*, followed by the words of Scripture, the first one of which was: *Man[4] shall not live by bread alone, but by every word that comes from the mouth of God* (Matthew 4:4).

These words show our personal need of the word of God for our lives today. They also show us that the word of God is verbal and inspired, written Scripture, preserved for all time.

---

3   As for instance, in *Totally Sufficient* (see footnote 2).
4   The Bible often refers to 'man' in this generic sense, which includes both men and women.

As well as upholding the divine authority of the Old Testament, Jesus made it clear that his own word was of equal authority, when he claimed to be the central fulfilment of those Scriptures. He said, *Do not think that I have come to abolish the Law or the Prophets; I have not come to abolish them but to fulfil them. For truly, I say to you, until heaven and earth pass away, not an iota, not a dot, will pass from the Law until all is accomplished* (Matthew 5:17–18). Jesus also said: *Heaven and earth will pass away, but my words will not pass away* (Matthew 24:35).

Such claims include the divine authority of his teaching. Speaking of Jesus, one biblical writer confirmed: *in these last days he* [God] *has spoken to us by his Son, whom he appointed the heir of all things, through whom also he created the world* (Hebrews 1:2).

Supreme authority

In that light, the Bible is the word of God. Possessing full divine authority, it is supremely relevant to our lives. Secular theories have no role in the re-interpretation of Scripture in the effort, made at times, to shape it to fit modern thought. Such must always be evaluated in the light of God's word.

> Secular theories have no role in the re-interpretation of Scripture in the effort, made at times, to shape it to fit modern thought

Only there do we find the context of fear and anxiety in the troubled world we have inherited, as well as our sinful, rebel nature in need of God's forgiveness. Jesus was very direct when he said: *Those who are well have no need of a physician, but those who are sick. I have not come to call the righteous but sinners to repentance* (Luke 5:31–32).

Again, Jesus is central, for, *the sacred writings ... are able to make you wise for salvation through faith in Christ Jesus* (2 Timothy 3:15). Then, in addition to that most vital wisdom, the Bible is completely sufficient to teach, correct and equip us for the challenges of a life trusting in God.

That is because *all Scripture is breathed out by God and profitable for teaching, for reproof, for correction, and for training in righteousness, that the man of God may be complete, equipped for every good work* (2 Timothy 3:16–17). God's clear and enlightening word covers all of life's situations, temptations, choices, trials and death itself, in fact, *all things that pertain to life and godliness through the knowledge of him who called us to his own glory and excellence* (2 Peter 1:3).

The Bible is realistic about life's troubles. But keep in mind that Jesus' teaching on anxiety and fear is not offered as a stand-alone remedy for those experiences. However, when such fears are seen in light of what the Bible teaches about our need for peace with God, and we personally trust in Christ, there is definite scope for facing our fears. Finding peace with God through personal trust in Christ comes first. Then, we have new resources to deal with any other troubling fears.

> **The Bible is realistic about life's troubles**

Encouragements

Jesus gave direct teaching on anxiety and fear to encourage his followers: *do not be anxious about your life, what you will eat or what you will drink, nor about your body, what you will put on ... Look at the birds of the air; they neither sow nor reap nor gather into barns, and yet your heavenly Father feeds them ... and clothes the grass of the field ... Therefore do not be anxious about tomorrow, for tomorrow will be anxious for itself. Sufficient for the day is its own trouble* (Matthew 6:25–34). Trust the fatherly care of God each day, who feeds the birds and clothes the fields with wild lilies and grass, and you will have no need to be eaten up with anxiety or nagging worry.

Then, to encourage his followers facing hostility, Jesus said, *So have no fear of them ... And do not fear those who kill the body but cannot kill the soul. Rather fear him who can destroy both soul and body in hell. Are not two sparrows sold for a penny? And not one of them will fall to the ground apart from your Father. But even the hairs of your head are all numbered. Fear not, therefore; you are of more value than many sparrows* (Matthew 10:26–31).

What fear-banishing teaching, but also what healthy fear-encouraging words! Don't miss God's loving care of his children. No detail is too small for his all-sufficient care. Trust him and have no fear!

Trust

Jesus also used a similar strong word for 'fear' (from which our word 'phobia' comes from the Greek) for the fitting attitude to God, who has full authority over hell itself. But, notice the difference between the two ways 'fear' is used: negatively, in hearts filled with thoughts of hostile opposition; but positively, of awe-filled reverence for God's person and authority in view of the great value he places upon his children.

Reverence God in this positive way that honours him and you will have little else to fear. That is the sense given in, *The fear of the LORD is the beginning of wisdom* (Proverbs 9:10). If my personal trust is in God, I am able to say: *The LORD is my light and my salvation; whom shall I fear? The LORD is the stronghold of my life; of whom shall I be afraid?* (Psalm 27:1).

God gives the calm certainty of his rescue and a generous supply of help in difficulties. He offers strong defence against those who may intend to cause our worst fears.

The Apostle Paul encourages Christians with: *For you did not receive the spirit of slavery to fall back into fear, but you have received the Spirit of adoption as sons, by whom we cry, 'Abba! Father!'* (Romans 8:15).

Faith, a personal trust in Christ, frees us from the ruling power of sin and from fear of judgement, as the gift of God's Holy Spirit gives sonship to God's children, with the high honour of calling him 'Father'.

Challenges

Paul also encouraged young Timothy, his fellow-worker in the gospel with these words: *for God gave us a spirit not of fear but of power and love and self-control* (2 Timothy 1:7). God's strength, his love, and the self-control given by the Holy Spirit, enable us to master timidity, worry and self-doubt. As Christians learn, day by day, to apply these truths by prayerful trust, we begin to overcome our crippling fears.

If some of these are phobias, perhaps linked with obsessive personality traits, overcoming them may need help from someone experienced in building confidence to face fears, so that they begin to become a lot more manageable. As well as 'obsessive' being a word used in secular psychology, it also describes a trait that has biblical examples.

Any pattern of thinking that becomes habitual may develop into an obsessive addiction to various behaviours like alcohol dependence, comfort eating, pornography, anger, gambling, substance abuse, laziness, workplace theft, smartphone addiction, false beliefs, and excuse-making, to name a few examples.

> Any pattern of thinking that becomes habitual may develop into an obsessive addiction

Did you ever hear the excuses, 'Oh, that's just the way I am,' or, 'God made me that way'? To all such excuses God's word exposes the heart of the problem: *The iniquities of the wicked ensnare him, and he is held fast in the cords of his sin* (Proverbs 5:22). Jesus confirmed that when he said, *everyone who practises sin is a slave to sin* (John 8:34).

It is unlikely that anyone suddenly becomes obsessive. What generally happens is that anxiety and stressful situations feed and accelerate a tendency that becomes established as a learned behaviour.

Addiction

There are many biblical accounts which show the addictive power of particular sins that conquered people's thinking and ruled their lives. These are given in God's word to teach us the devastating effects of sin, which cry out for a divine solution.

Consider the following biblical examples. The first is of repetitive behaviour in the form of religious addiction to alluring false beliefs in heathen worship, as we see it in the life of Manasseh.

As well as a king, this man was also a slave, bound to his false beliefs and the inevitable behaviours that followed them, when *he did what was*

*evil in the sight of the Lord, according to the despicable practices of the
nations ... he rebuilt the high places ... he erected altars for Baal ... and
worshipped all the host of heaven and served them ... and used fortune-
telling and omens and dealt with mediums and with necromancers*[5]
(2 Kings 21:2–6).

Superstition and moral weakness

Manasseh was duped by the lying propaganda of Satan, which
masquerades as the 'wisdom' behind all false religious and secular
philosophical beliefs. He was convinced that his beliefs were vital to his
success, but driving them all was his bondage to superstitious fear.
However, later in life the good news is that God was very merciful to
him and changed even Manasseh, when he was humbled and asked for
God's help—*Then Manasseh knew that the LORD was God*
(2 Chronicles 33:13).

Then take strong-man Samson and his impulsive relationships with a
succession of women, including Delilah, who quickly gained power over
him by her cajoling on behalf of Samson's enemies, the Philistines. We
soon see how Samson's moral weakness was exploited by her repetitive
acts of scheming and of his yielding to the enslaving power of sin. Later,
cruelly blinded by his enemies, and forced to work in the prison grinding
mill, poor Samson became a degraded spectacle given to warn us to avoid
his foolish behaviour (see Judges chapter 16).

Whatever it is, all sin is offensive to God, so
we must turn from it all in genuine sorrow and
turn back to him, seeking his forgiveness through
Christ. The daily challenge for the Christian is to
continue to turn away from the old thought-life
to our new life in Christ, so that, *If we live by
the Spirit, let us also keep in step with the Spirit*
(Galatians 5:25).

> All sin is offensive
> to God, so we must
> turn from it all in
> genuine sorrow and
> back to him, seeking
> his forgiveness
> through Christ

---

5 Necromancy refers to the practice of using witchcraft and sorcery.

Progress

This is a lifetime exercise, *For those who live according to the flesh set their minds on the things of the flesh, but those who live according to the Spirit set their minds on the things of the Spirit* (Romans 8:5). The 'flesh' refers to our sinful nature, which affects every part of our lives. This includes the thoughts, sometimes stirred by anxious worry and fear, that lead to habitual actions, and slowly but surely to life-styles.

This reminds us of how some illness may be caused, for instance, by severe anxiety, and how the mind closely interacts with the body in a 'psychosomatic' (mind/body) relationship.

The Bible speaks about the 'heart' as our mind and will corrupted by sin, as in, *The heart is deceitful above all things, and desperately sick; who can understand it?* (Jeremiah 17:9). Or, as in personal responsibility: *Keep your heart with all vigilance, for from it flow the springs of life* (Proverbs 4:23), and in the need of our whole person to: *Trust in the LORD with all your heart and do not lean on your own understanding* (Proverbs 3:5).

We have seen how anxious fears result from a broken relationship with God. A lot of these fears also spill into our minds from our living in a fearful, uncertain world far from God.

Anxious fears result from a broken relationship with God

Is the Bible sufficient for all these issues of personal and practical living? Yes, absolutely—even today.

4. Guilt and anxiety— roots of fear

I f fear is a response to thoughts or situations that trigger it, what is the root cause of all these thoughts? This is where the word of God gives us the answer and hope for the worst of fears.

Personal

The Bible reveals that we are more than physical matter. In Genesis we see a relationship between our humanity, created in the image of God, and our reason and thinking. In fact, Genesis shows that men and women were the magnificent crown of God's personal creation, when *God said, 'Let us make man in our image, after our likeness'* (Genesis 1:26).

The way God is related by creation to men and women is indicated in the words 'image' and 'likeness'. These show that our humanity was created with a personal nature that in some amazing, non-physical, ways resembled God himself.

Although Adam and Eve stood far below God, their unique persons were truly related to their personal Creator. They were conscious, rational, and moral persons; the frail, finite image of God, who is spirit.

As such, they were exalted persons made for eternity with God. But then Eve fell under the subtle deception of Satan, an influential evil spirit full of hostile malignity towards God.

Then, after they had both disobeyed God, *they heard the sound of the LORD God walking in the garden in the cool of the day, and the man and his wife hid themselves from the presence of the LORD God among the trees of the garden. But the LORD God called to the man and said to him, 'Where are you?'* (Genesis 3:8–9).

Chapter 4

Broken

They heard God's searching question and tried to hide. Before they had rejected God, he had spoken to them and had warned them directly, that if they chose to disobey him—*you shall surely die* (Genesis 2:17). But now, their friendship with God was broken. Alarmed, they were overcome with the urgent need to escape from the cause of such dread. This then is the origin of that most basic fear—the guilty fear of God's personal displeasure and judgement.

When Adam and Eve rejected God, they were left without a chart or compass, facing real fears and great uncertainty about life and what it would mean to die. This again is the origin of our psychological problems—and everyone has some, varying in type and severity.

Trapped

Now, the pair lived for their own goals and dreams in an abnormal reality, but rather than finding true freedom, they found an existence in which they were condemned to fear, decay and death. When they rejected God's wisdom, their own new false 'wisdom' became their futile attempt to create their own enlightenment.

> Rather than finding true freedom, they found an existence in which they were condemned to fear, decay and death

What they thought was freedom became corrupted phantasies that somehow they hoped would offer a new world with high adventure. Instead, disobedience had changed their relationship with God, and also changed their nature, beyond their recovery, to one marked by foolish malice towards God, and often towards one another.

This biblical analysis opens a window on our present self-knowledge, on our rebel humanity under God's judgement, and our deception which brings fearful and futile thinking.

This catastrophe includes us all. Thinking it is all good, natural and wise—we inherit Adam's folly and his fears. For we are all the direct descendants of the first human pair, and need to face that: *therefore, just as sin came into the world through one man, and death through sin, and so death spread to all men because all sinned* (Romans 5:12). So, it is no surprise to find people today fearful of death and being trapped in an unwanted, oppressive eternity.

Diagnosis

The Genesis, real-time, historic 'fall' is up-to-date with its diagnosis of our worst ills: self-willed disobedience of God and our rejection of him. Today, Genesis remains vital for understanding our greatest problems.

One of the catastrophic results of evolutionary belief is that it can never explain why things are as bad as they are. The next chapter will help you to see why evolution offers no insight into our human origin, our true moral guilt, fear, hatred, violence and the longing for wholeness and meaning.

Indeed, some anxious thoughts are the effects of conscience, which marks our responsibility to God and challenges us to preserve a semblance of right and wrong in the preservation of human society by upholding God-given justice, law and order.

> The image of God is a deep fact of our humanity ... all attempts to eradicate it ... only dehumanise us further

What the secular project wants to ignore is that the image of God is a deep fact of our humanity and that all attempts to eradicate it do not lead to social progress but only dehumanise us further. As a result we become hopeless, fearful and degraded in thought and action.

The Apostle Paul knew the moral state of mankind both from the word of God and from what he had seen in his many journeys to the cities of the Roman Empire. He describes, with devastating realism, how: *They are darkened in their understanding, alienated from the life of God because of the ignorance that is in them, due to their hardness of heart. They have become callous and have given themselves up to sensuality, greedy to practice every kind of impurity* (Ephesians 4:18–19).

Reality

Now you know why people are still so troubled, and why only the word of God reveals the reality of deep human failure and fear. It alone has clear, final answers for the basis of knowledge, love, personal being, truth and meaning, guilt and forgiveness, compared with evolutionary beliefs and secular social science.

It also has an answer for life and death, for a meaningful origin in a personal Creator, for the origin of humanity, for broken personalities and a broken world. It also has the answer for fear.

Jesus gave a very direct challenge about human thinking, when he taught: *from within, out of the heart of man, come evil thoughts, sexual immorality, theft, murder, adultery, coveting, wickedness, deceit, sensuality, envy, slander, pride, foolishness* (Mark 7:21–22).

With his heart-searching diagnosis of the moral state of the human heart, we are left in no doubt that all such sins, including evil thoughts, are offensive to God. By nature we are all morally ruined and corrupted, completely unprepared to face the challenge of eternity.

> By nature we are all morally ruined and corrupted, completely unprepared to face the challenge of eternity

Despite the fact that so many lives are being torn apart by these same sinful life-styles and ruined by stress, anger and anxiety, today it has become a tragic sort of secular normality. No, this is not normality; it is the result of living as defiant rebels against God. In fact, we are all now *hostile in mind, doing evil deeds* (Colossians 1:21). In all the dark confusion and fear, many look to find relief in alcohol, drugs, false optimism, and confused relationships. Some become ensnared by the occult in a dangerous attempt to find harmony with *the cosmic powers over this present darkness* (Ephesians 6:12), while others turn to meditation-based practices.

False relief

Oh, not so fast—all such pseudo-escapes are doomed. Those who follow them pay a heavy price in psychological problems—changed moods and anxiety, self-absorption, futile attempts to raise self-esteem, troubled relationships and depression, including many fears.

For many the challenge of this 'real' reality check of true moral guilt before God comes as a shock, but whether shock or not, now is the time to face God's verdict. For all these sins are marks of our deep alienation from God. They are like the proverbial tip of the iceberg that points beneath to the reality of a far worse problem—*for all have sinned and fall short of the glory of God* (Romans 3:23).

But how will God ever uphold his own moral rule and just verdict and at the same time forgive undeserving rebels? This is what makes the love of God revealed in the cross of Christ such astonishing good news. God's final answer is only found in the death of Christ, when he took God's just punishment upon himself that the sins of others deserved and died in their place to rescue them from an eternal condemnation.

Escape

Today, the one way back to God is freely accessible: Jesus said, *I am the door. If anyone enters by me, he will be saved* (John 10:9). No, this is not a multiple-choice option—*God sent his only Son into the world, so that we might live through him* (1 John 4:9).

Carefully consider these issues. This may be the time to admit that the fearful thoughts of an empty eternity may have become habitual, caused by an anxious uncertainty about the future. God has written the law of moral cause and effect into human thought and action. We reap what we sow. Behind the fear of eternity is the fear of meeting Almighty God as Judge.

> God has written the law of moral cause and effect into human thought and action

These fears challenge us to turn to the gospel of Christ, where we find how unsettling fears may be replaced by love, peace and joy. God has made our humanity a union of body and soul, so some fear of eternity may also have to do with our shrinking from an unnatural disembodied existence after death.

In a later chapter we look at how the fear of being a disembodied soul in eternity is resolved by faith in Christ and a bodily resurrection.

If you think of eternity as a blank emptiness that grips you, maybe it is time to accept that God, in person, is present everywhere. Even the *highest heaven cannot contain* (2 Chronicles 6:18) his personal glory and majesty. We also need to face the challenge that without personal faith in Christ, *whoever does not believe is condemned already* (John 3:18).

Cause and effect

This is why we need to turn away from false and confused beliefs, and repent of all our sins—in thoughts and actions. There is one very good reason for doing this: for *now he* [God] *commands all people everywhere to repent* (Acts 17:30). That means we must confess all our sins to God. We must turn from them and ask God to forgive them all.

Then, with God's forgiveness we receive peace and a confident trust in Jesus as we learn to go on trusting him, replacing fears with new thoughts and attitudes of peace and joy.

In this new life, in a living relationship with the Lord Jesus, he gives us his own strong encouragements: *Peace I leave with you; my peace I give to you. Not as the world gives do I give to you. Let not your hearts be troubled, neither let them be afraid* (John 14:27). With such a promise, we need to deal with a serious question.

5. Can Darwin help?

Today, Darwin is relevant because so many rely on Neo-Darwinism for their belief in origins. For them, evolution is a natural process that debunks special creation by God. Neo-Darwinism integrates the science of genetics within Darwin's evolutionary framework, and forms the foundation for how much of the West understands human identity and behaviour. So, perhaps you ask, can I combine Jesus' teaching with Darwin's insights to help me overcome serious fear?

Discovery

Charles Darwin was socially well-connected. After university he had an amazing opportunity to join an important British naval survey expedition on *HMS Beagle* as an unpaid naturalist.

While not a professional naturalist, he was an acute observer and saw many fascinating creatures during the period 1831-1835 at various places on the long sea voyages. Many of the birds and animals he described were on the isolated islands of the Galápagos in the Pacific Ocean, off the coast of South America. In other places he also found fossils of large extinct animals. Darwin knew that many ideas, at that time of social progress, were in a ferment, and he had thoughts of change.

The proposal was already well-known that human life was organically connected in a chain to all living creatures, where higher forms had evolved over aeons by many gradual steps from lower forms.

Origins

Based on his observations, Darwin developed a theory of evolution by natural selection, which was published in 1859 under the title, as commonly abbreviated, 'On the Origin of Species'. Agnosticism towards Christianity had a strong influence on Darwin's new beliefs and many found his new ideas about human origins very appealing. With such natural processes behind life and its development there seemed no need for special creation by God.

But now, looking back we see a subtle twist, for when he assumed the truth of his theory, he hadn't seen how it would undermine the validity of his own thinking. We see this when he was reflecting that the universe was not the result of chance, but then admitted his doubt. In 1881, one year before he died, he wrote to William Graham:

But then with me the horrid doubt always arises whether the convictions of man's mind, which has been developed from the mind of the lower animals, are of any value or at all trustworthy. Would anyone trust in the convictions of a monkey's mind, if there are any convictions in such a mind?[6]

By the time he had seen that conclusion, likely without recognising the full impact of it, he had undermined his trust in his own theory, which relied on the evidence of his observations interpreted by a naturalistic world-view. Whether he saw it or not, his new beliefs downgraded his own reasoning that he had used to form those very same beliefs.

> Whether he saw it or not, his new beliefs downgraded his own reasoning that he had used to form those very same beliefs

A rejection of God's creation of the first human pair as personal image-bearers of God and his reliance on naturalistic error led Darwin into futile and dehumanising thinking. Despite that, some still try to combine Jesus' teaching with Darwin's ideas, but it is like trying to mix light with darkness. This combination is often called 'theistic evolution', which questions Adam as a real historical person, and usually denies a literal Genesis Fall into sin, which then undermines the need for Christ's sin-bearing death on the cross. Avoid the confusion of serious compromise—and be clear as to why you should.

---

6 https://www.darwinproject.ac.uk/letter/DCP-LETT-13230.xml

Conflict

Darwin's new system of belief rested on some genuine observations but interpreted by serious error. He made his observations using his high view of reason, which was the legacy of his education, but also without acknowledging it as a person made in the image of God.

But then, using his prior commitment to naturalistic error as his new authority to interpret his findings left him with a 'horrid doubt', not able fully to trust his convictions developed from lower animals. Whether or not he had written about his doubt, the central beliefs put forward in his theory are false and downgrade the validity of all human reason.

His rejection of God's word about special creation led to his deception that his mind had come from lower animals. Despite that, many believe his theory has the hallmarks of science and proof. After all, Darwin believed he had ample evidence for his theory, like variations in the related species of bird's beaks, and other similar variations.

Was he right? How do we assess these many types of variation?

We now know such variations show that in the same genetic pool there is potential for creatures to adapt quite quickly to changes such as diet and climate, and that these observable differences may lead scientists to classify creatures as distinct species.

Only rarely do adaptability and speciation take place by chance mutations acting with natural selection to confer advantages, but even then, such mutations are impotent to create new kinds of creatures. Most observable changes are due to the way creatures express pre-existing genetic information in different environments. As it is, mutations never add genetic information, only scrambled loss.

Darwin lived before an appreciation of the role of mutations and genetics. But as he formed his theory, he always explained his findings so they agreed with his theory. This made it sound so plausible that it seemed to offer a science-based replacement for biblical Christianity.

> Biblical Christianity supports genuine science; it is intellectually defensible and invites careful enquiry

Has science proven Darwin's theory and discredited Christianity? Not at all: biblical Christianity supports genuine science; it is intellectually defensible and invites careful enquiry. What happened was this: when Darwin rejected God's truth revealed in Genesis and believed his mind had developed from monkeys, the high view of reason he had used when proposing his new beliefs was completely falsified by those same new beliefs.

Light shines

Any rejection of God's word inevitably leads a person to believe whatever sounds plausible to them—and for that they have no excuse. If you believe in Darwinian evolution from a single cell in a chain to human life, you have no basis for trusting the thinking by which you accepted those beliefs. You have fallen into self-contradictory thinking.

The ideas sound plausible, but the organic chain linking an accidental original living cell to our humanity never happened. It was scientism;[7] wishful thinking based on naturalism that tried to explain life without the Genesis account of creation, a God-given understandable cosmos, and the bedrock truths of the life, death and resurrection of Jesus.

So, despite all the efforts of unbelief to extinguish the light of Christ, the effort has never succeeded, and instead, *the light shines in the darkness, and the darkness has not overcome it* (John 1:5).

In sharp contrast, Darwin's scheme leaves us as degraded animals with an accidental origin in a pool of chemicals on a journey to nowhere. Evolution offers no meaning to life, and no answers for the real evil we all face. Of course Darwin didn't set out to deceive anyone, but his provocative, widely published false beliefs were intended to replace God's revealed truth, which inevitably led to his dark self-deception.

> Darwin's scheme leaves us as degraded animals with an accidental origin in a pool of chemicals on a journey to nowhere

7 Scientism is the ideology of a prior commitment to naturalistic science that believes, without warrant, that the only truth is scientific truth.

A question

The upshot of all this leaves you with one of the most serious questions you will ever face. Who will you believe: the living creator God, who cannot lie, who says *I am the LORD, and there is no other … I made the earth and created man on it* (Isaiah 45:6 and 45:12), or Charles Darwin, who rejected God's revealed truth and condemned his own thinking in the process—and yours if you believe him?

Of course, if you believe Darwin, you still retain the high gift of reason, but you misuse it, in unbelief, to defy God and believe God-dishonouring error. The consequences are never neutral. If you believe your faculty of reason has come from lower animals, that false belief condemns you to the secular devaluation of your human identity.

Darwin's theory has no answer for the deep problems of humanity. Rather it has directly facilitated the now dominant Western secular humanism, hand in hand with atheism and, as a consequence, accelerated the wide-scale moral collapse we see today into deeper decadence, corruption, anxiety, violence and fear.

God's word is clear: *since they did not see fit to acknowledge God, God gave them up to a debased mind to do what ought not to be done* (Romans 1:28). The end result of all this is not progress, but a long list of wretched trouble, which includes, *evil, covetousness, malice … envy, murder, strife, deceit … they are … foolish, faithless, heartless, ruthless* (Romans 1:29–31).

We don't need to look too far in society to see it, do we?

Darwin offers no help to a true understanding of the origin of life, of true moral failure and guilt, fear or death. He is of no help in facing the challenge of eternity.

> Darwin … is of no help in facing the challenge of eternity

When considering a serious challenge, it makes sense to face the facts.

6. Facts of fear

In the face of widespread moral trouble and real fear, let's look at some of the types of fear seen in some well-known Bible characters. As well as anxiety about eternity, there are many other fears that grip people's minds. Here is a brief look at various fears, and how to face them.

Realism

Jesus accepted the reality of fear and how it often controls people's minds and their lives. He knew its origin back in the moral rebellion recorded in Genesis and the way forward for those trapped by it.

He also knew the Scriptures and that, as the Son of God, he was their guarantor, standing over them all as God's inspired word.

He confirmed his own central role in God's purpose when, after his resurrection, he said to his close followers, *These are my words that I spoke to you while I was still with you, that everything written about me in the Law of Moses and the Prophets and the Psalms must be fulfilled* (Luke 24:44). Jesus is central in the three sections of Scripture he mentioned that cover all of the thirty-nine books of the Old Testament as published today. Here are some accounts about fear, with which Jesus was familiar.

Insight

These various angles on fear may give you some insight into your own. Many fears are completely understandable. If you are in an abusive relationship,

> **Many fears are completely understandable**

or fearful about the loss of your job or about a serious illness, all these things are common causes of anxiety or fear. However, some people really do feel overwhelmed by their fears.

King Solomon once prayed that God would answer all who asked for his help, *each knowing his own affliction and his own sorrow*

(2 Chronicles 6:29), that God would forgive them and that they would turn to live in his ways. Affliction and sorrow are universal. No one escapes them.

Trouble

Here are some people who faced anxiety, dread, horror and panic.

Twice in the many journeys of Abram (later called Abraham) and his wife Sarai or Sarah, Abraham feared for his life at the hand of foreign rulers, on account of the very attractive looks of his wife. Quite simply, he was alarmed that the rulers would take his wife by force and remove him by death, and so to secure his safety Abraham's ploy was to lie that she was not his wife but his sister. This actually got him into quite serious trouble (see Genesis 12:10–20).

While Abraham's fear boils down to the fear of a violent death, it was the social pressure that motivated him to lie so as to escape from his rational fear. Abraham is not alone. Many have tried lying and other foolish moves to remove or conceal the cause of their guilty fear. Don't let your guilty fears destroy you, but seek God's forgiveness.

> Don't let your guilty fears destroy you, but seek God's forgiveness

Joseph's older brothers were envious of him as their father's favourite, and one day saw their opportunity to get rid of him. Far from home, they took Joseph's lovingly-gifted coat and sold the teenager to traders on their way to Egypt. They bloodied the coat and returned to their father with the tale that Joseph had been killed by a wild animal. Their father Jacob was understandably heartbroken.

Many guilty and fearful people tell lies easily, but what a tangled web they produce, at times producing intense anxiety of being found out.

Purpose

As it turned out, God had a purpose in this. Years later, after many trials, at a time of widespread famine, Joseph had risen to great prominence in

Egypt, when the Pharaoh placed him over the huge grain storage project and the subsequent international sales of grain.

Then, when Joseph's brothers were sent to Egypt to buy grain they were perplexed by the manner of the striking individual in charge of grain sales. This is an emotion-packed story of the brothers facing Joseph in an extraordinary reversal of power. In his earlier trials God had taught Joseph to be forgiving, but years later on the death of their father, the brothers were fearful that Joseph would get his revenge.

Pity these fearful brothers in awe of Joseph's authority in Egypt, but be challenged by Joseph's words to them: *'you meant evil against me, but God meant it for good, to bring about that many people should be kept alive, as they are today. So do not fear; I will provide for you and your little ones.' Thus he comforted them and spoke kindly to them* (Genesis 50:20–21).

Guilt

The social fears in this turbulent true story are seen in the brothers' guilty fears of one day having their lies to their grief-stricken father found out. Then there is their fear of Joseph in his high rank in Egypt, the world superpower. Later, there is their alarm at the prospect of Joseph's reprisal, for he could have easily had them all thrown into a dark prison cell and left in tormented squalor for the rest of their days.

These fears are dealt with by Joseph's forgiving attitude, as he tells his brothers 'do not fear' and perhaps also by his father's forbearance of his sons' earlier deception. We will only learn such forgiveness when we ask Joseph's God to forgive our own sins. For just at the right time, God freely gave up his own Son, the Lord Jesus Christ, to bear the penalty of others' sins, so that they might be forgiven, and the fearful reconciled to the God of peace.

There are many other Bible stories in which fear plays a strong role. Here are two more: the early relationship of David and King Saul, and then in the New Testament, where we see fear in the life of the Apostle Paul, who was not afraid to write about it.

Saul was the first king of Israel, who had a very determined, cold and somewhat harsh and unstable personality. At times he was rash, and lacked foresight. His early military campaigns centred more on his personal prestige than on national success, and he suffered from dark mood swings into bouts of depression and jealous anger, which he relieved by the soothing strains of young David's lyre playing.

Courage

But after David's courageous victory over Goliath the Philistine giant, when even the whole army had been panic-stricken by this huge man, David became a national hero. Then, after his further military success we read: *Saul eyed David from that day on* (1 Samuel 18:9). Saul's depressive episodes then became very challenging for young David.

The king even took to trying to pin him to the wall with a javelin during the lyre-playing sessions, when David cleverly evaded death.

After this *Saul was afraid of David because the LORD was with him but had departed from Saul* (1 Samuel 18:12). Saul had foolishly disobeyed God and it was only a matter of time before David became king.

In Saul we see a depressed and jealous fear of David, who showed Saul great respect and who never tried to take the kingship by force. Saul's life challenges us to avoid his proud, vicious and self-centred life.

If you have deep-seated personality difficulties, consider locating a pastor or biblical counsellor to help you. At times, we try to bury guilt. Be sure to face it, confess it to God and seek his forgiveness.

Affliction

Finally, we note the Apostle Paul, once Saul of Tarsus, the persecutor of Christians, who met the ascended Christ and thereafter spread the good news of Christ and faced much opposition for doing so. He described it like this: *In all our affliction, I am overflowing with joy. For even when we came to Macedonia, our bodies had no rest, but we were afflicted at every turn—fighting without and fear within. But God, who comforts the downcast, comforted us by the coming of Titus* (2 Corinthians 7:4–6). There is the word 'affliction' again; 'distress, trouble and pressure' that Solomon mentioned in his prayer. We all know about it.

The Apostle had hostile enemies, but even when he faced civil unrest he was careful to work within the freedoms granted by Roman law. His words 'fighting without and fear within' refer to how, at times, opposition caused him to fear. Paul is realistic. He knew the threats; he had been hauled before authorities and beaten, even stoned by an angry mob; and he could write of how he was so encouraged by the caring visit of a fellow-worker.

Prayer

Paul knew the great resource of prayer, of encouragement from close friends, and from the confidence and joy that God the Holy Spirit gave his heart and mind. Once, when he needed fresh courage in his challenging mission, God spoke to him in the night, *Do not be afraid, but go on speaking and do not be silent, for I am with you* (Acts 18:9–10). Paul understood fear. He never pretended it didn't exist, but he knew the presence of God, and did not let fears overwhelm his mind.

> Paul understood fear. He never pretended it didn't exist, but he knew the presence of God, and did not let fears overwhelm his mind

In these accounts, people's fears are opened up for us: some to offer practical help, including loving Christian friendship, but some are fears to avoid. Fear covers many things, such as the fear of death, God's final judgement, social rejection, loss of loved ones, disease, and hostile anger inflicting brutal beatings, and insecurity.

A lot of fear is negative, but, as we saw earlier, positive fear means the reverence of God that replaces cowering fear with amazed awe at being loved, accepted and forgiven, as in, *The fear of the LORD is the beginning of wisdom; all those who practice it have good understanding* (Psalm 111:10).

Many have found great comfort from God's promises found in the Psalms, which Christians often use in public worship. In them we see how God answers prayer, as in these poignant words: *I cry out to God Most High, to God who fulfils his purpose for me* (Psalm 57:2).

Peace

Jesus knew the future world events, and foretold worldwide trouble, worry and anxiety about the future close to his return in universal majesty. He said that there would be *distress of nations in perplexity because of the roaring sea and the waves, people fainting with fear and with foreboding of what is coming on the world* (Luke 21:25–26).

Today, we live in a fear-filled world. Some fears are complex. Share your fears with a sympathetic listener. Don't build a hard exterior to conceal fear. Turn to Christ for the forgiveness of your sins. Trust in God, who comes alongside the weak, enabling them to say: *The LORD is on my side; I will not fear. What can man do to me?* (Psalm 118:6).

But perhaps you are still holding out, hoping to find some other refuge that human self-confidence has left in its potential. Let's see.

> We live in a fear-filled world. Some fears are complex. Share your fears with a sympathetic listener. Don't build a hard exterior to conceal fear

7. Atheism? — No fear!

Many believe that atheism has got rid of their fears of eternity; while others prefer atheism to religion when they see a world full of trouble. How does atheism deal with fear? Can you trust the answer?

Unscientific?

New atheism is popularised by Richard Dawkins, Peter Atkins, Sam Harris and Daniel Dennett, to name a few; men who are sure that science underpins their beliefs. For them, any belief in God is foolish faith in the supernatural. Do we have a reasoned reply? This discussion covers: science, the validity of human reason, and the problem of evil.

Some believe atheism gets rid of all their fears of God as Judge. If materialism is true, then God is no more. But if everything is physical matter how does human thinking, being merely the accidental product of matter plus time plus chance, know that materialism is true? Ultimately, its followers choose to believe it. In this context, materialism is a 'belief' that denies the existence of God, and believes that an accidental big bang origin of the cosmos is a rational explanation.

> If everything is physical matter how does human thinking, being merely the accidental product of matter plus time plus chance, know that materialism is true?

But thinking and logic work remarkably well. Science has produced amazing results, which lead atheists to believe their position is secure. All this is achieved without any belief in God. Conceal the leap of 'blind trust' in materialism, and the case for atheism may look strong, until we consider thinking itself. Then, we meet some large challenges.

Accident or created wonder?

Early modern science was developed by researchers, many of whom understood their rationality to be a finite reflection of the mind of God the creator. Atheists assume those beliefs were superstitious. However, many in the early modern scientific enterprise believed that reality was neither an accident, nor a cosmic dream, but a real created wonder, and that the cosmos was rich in information, much of it discoverable. These new methods of science assumed a Christian view of creation, involving an understandable universe, careful research, integrity, rational evidence and repeatable experiments. This foundation led to great advances and has become the legacy inherited by modern science, giving the success we enjoy today. Aeroplanes fly, computers work and medical science has brought huge advances as well as many ethical challenges.

'If the whole universe has no meaning, we should never have found out it has no meaning.'

Of course, atheists reject the biblical base and believe that a truly free humanity has no need for God. But that view rests on an inconsistent foundation, some of which is unavoidably based on the legacy of the tested biblical truths, and some on the secular denials of that legacy.

The result is a paradox that C. S. Lewis noted: 'If the whole universe has no meaning, we should never have found out it has no meaning.'[8] But as atheism believes the whole universe has no final meaning, however could that 'truth' of no meaning be discovered in a universe devoid of all meaning? That must get close to the ultimate paradox.

Reason

Atheism has no evidence-based findings to show how reasoned thought has come from physical matter

If everything is physical or material, atheism has no evidence-based findings to show how reasoned thought has come from physical

8   C. S. Lewis, *Mere Christianity* (© C. S. Lewis Pte. Ltd. 1952) p. 42.

matter. The new atheist Sam Harris has studied neuroscience which, based on his philosophical materialism, relies on evolution and various theories to explain the conscious mind. But then, if our thinking has arrived on the basis of physical matter plus time plus chance, this scheme can hardly defend atheism, when all it has to depend on is a complex physical, molecular-based reasoning process inherited from animals.

The big challenge for the atheist is our conscious person and mind, which are so complex that they defy his or her prior commitment to an accidental, evolutionary origin. Jesus made the special creation of humanity clear when, speaking about marriage, he said *that he who created them from the beginning made them male and female* (Matthew 19:4).

We have been created *in the image of God* (Genesis 1:27). In our personal make-up, we already know about our creation by God, which according to the Bible we suppress, hoping to avoid being confronted by it. The result is that, by nature, all people, not only atheists, *became futile in their thinking* (Romans 1:21).

Reality

Atheism assumes a naturalistic world-view. So when atheists say their belief is science-based, they mean that the whole of reality is physical matter and follows the laws of physics and science—it is all natural.

The question remains: is a mindless accidental explosion a sufficient basis for true information and conscious minds to appear? Atheists do not know how a human brain, even with its billions of neurons, knows about reality.

For all his brilliance in proposing the theory of relativity and much else, Albert Einstein became a pantheist (the whole cosmos, mind and matter is an impersonal god), but he could never fathom how he had discovered what was there in reality. He was left in bewildered amazement: 'The eternally incomprehensible thing about the world is its comprehensibility.'[9]

---

9   Albert Einstein, *Physics and Reality*, Journal of the Franklin Institute (Mar. 1936).

Why was he so baffled? Like an atheist, he assumed the legacy but denied an understandable universe created by the personal living God. So he was at a complete loss to know how the personal could ever appear and gain knowledge on the basis of a non-personal first cause.

Atheism (as well as pantheism) leaves people with no answers for their deep fears of non-being, or of the magnificence and terrible awesomeness of it all, and the searing anguish and pain of suffering, disease and death, and the terribleness of having personal being and rational minds, but trying to prop them up with hopelessness.

No hope

Listen to Peter Atkins describe what he thinks will happen when the sun dies: 'We shall have gone the journey of all purposeless stardust, driven unwittingly by chaos, gloriously but aimlessly evolved into sentience, born unchoosingly into the world, unwillingly taken from it, and inescapably returned to nothing.' [10] In the end his atheism and its eloquent-sounding despair offers no hope to the challenge of eternity.

> His atheism and its eloquent-sounding despair offers no hope to the challenge of eternity

How do atheists handle their idea of the nature of belief itself, which unlike physical matter does not have dimensions? Based on materialism, atheistic beliefs rise from electro-chemical mental processes in a futile attempt to deny God's existence. With such a basis for thinking, this must get close to being the ultimate enterprise of misguided reason, and it is certainly not science.

Ultimate

We have seen that the validity of reason, verifiable proof, honesty, meaning and truth, all flow from a Bible-based world-view. But atheism cannot

10 Peter Atkins, *On Being* (OUP, 2011), p. 100.

avoid 'borrowing' traits that mirror a belief in God—such as the validity of reason, an ultimate frame of reference (how else can they try to deny that God exists?), and ethical values. All are inconsistent with atheism, but 'borrowed' from our being made in the image of God.

An interesting thing about an atheist like Richard Dawkins is the way he uses science and reason to enhance the prestige of atheism—until we take a closer look.

Think about his observation: 'Science-fiction authors, such as Daniel. F. Galouye in *Counterfeit World*, have even suggested (and I cannot think how to disprove it) that we live in a computer simulation, set up by some vastly superior civilization.'[11] On his own assumptions, Dawkins was unable to disprove that his perception of reality may be fictional.

His atheistic view of reality has no evidence-based way of figuring out whether he is a computer-simulated 'Richard Dawkins' or a real Richard Dawkins in a truly significant reality—what a dilemma!

Reversed delusion

Dawkins' big goal is to show that the living God, especially of biblical Christianity, is a delusion, and that his atheism is the real final deal.

But this is the crunch: he admits he has no way of knowing whether he is in a real reality or a simulated one.

He's not sure if his atheism is part of the possible computer-simulated reality in which he finds himself. Clearly, he doesn't like that dilemma and prefers to fall back on what he doesn't want to admit: his true significance in a 'real reality', as a man made in the image of God.

Then, to avoid being cornered by that truth, he must conceal it to argue against the existence of God. He needs to do this to try to show he's dealing with objective reality and ultimate issues. Clearly, he prefers the 'borrowed' real reality, where he has valid rationality, or things look decidedly bleak if one is only a cypher in a computer simulation.

---

11 Richard Dawkins, *The God Delusion* (Bantam Press), 2006, p. 73.

Make believe

Richard Dawkins' make-believe world of a possible virtual sub-reality is the confused thinking that inevitably follows his denial of the living God, who *has scattered the proud in the thoughts of their hearts* (Luke 1:51). He then has the audacity to call God, the creator of this amazing reality, a 'delusion'. Don't you think by now the game is over?

If you do, that is only the first step. The next is to admit that atheism abandons reason, but that biblical Christianity alone gives a true assessment, when it says that, by nature, all live *in the futility of their minds. They are darkened in their understanding, alienated from the life of God because of the ignorance that is in them, due to their hardness of heart* (Ephesians 4:17–18). When you have accepted that as a divinely revealed description of your rebellion against God, your next step is of *repentance toward God and of faith in our Lord Jesus Christ* (Acts 20:21).

Atheistic beliefs are not consistent with atheism, because atheism can only rest human reason in neurons, and electro-chemistry, but has no basis for final truth to exist in an ultimately meaningless universe.

Explanation

Yes, the world is still in a terrible objective moral mess and Genesis has already given us the reason for that. We have already noted the Bible teaches that in our in hostile 'unrighteousness' against God, in our dark moral defiance, we *suppress the truth* (Romans 1:18).

> The world is still in a terrible objective moral mess and Genesis has already given us the reason for that

With that analysis we all know that God exists, but many struggle to keep that knowledge out of their minds. So, some have become atheists seeing the world, on one level, beautiful and astonishing, but on another, mired in cruelty, disease, fears and war, and they draw a flawed conclusion based on their sense of justice and morality.

They reject the biblical account of a historic moral fall into our state of rebellion against God, now marked by so much trouble, and accept the false belief of evolution. With their eyes shut to the truth, they still dislike the trouble. So they adopt the role of judges and pronounce that as a truly good and all-powerful God would never have made such a shocking mess, he could not possibly exist. Blind to their own moral rebellion against God, they still dislike all the trouble and evil, as they admit that so much seems to be wrong, and inadvertently agree with the truth of the Bible. Some atheists also argue against God's existence as if it was their worst fear, then try to deny his existence to get rid of their fears.

Discovery

Here is the atheist's big dilemma—was atheistic belief discoverable information? No, such beliefs take shape within personal minds. If there is no God, how would anyone have ever found out such a stunning piece of negative information? Well, you may say, 'Turn it around and assume God exists.' This is completely different—because only with the living God, whose existence we all know but naturally suppress, is there a sufficient explanation for why the cosmos also exists, and why we are awed by its grandeur. Now we also have a basis for the validity of reason, for personality, and, with the truths of Genesis, why everything is wonderful, beautiful, but seriously flawed.

> Only with the living God ... is there a sufficient explanation for why the cosmos exists ... and ... why everything is wonderful, beautiful, but seriously flawed

Wonderful

Now my understanding fits reality as it is, for with the Bible there is a solid basis for meaning and truth and personal communication. Now, the Creator has revealed why we exist: to reflect his person and glory, and for this world to be the arena to reveal his purpose in salvation and in the perfect New Creation. Atheists too need eternal life.

At its core, atheism is not science; it is a leap into the dark, an anti-biblical protest. On the other hand, biblical Christianity is defensible and consistent with its assumptions and beliefs, and with reality as it is, with our dilemmas, fears and difficulties. At the same time it is able to be lived out in practice—never perfectly, but very satisfyingly.

Atheists ridicule the Bible's meaning of 'faith' as if it were the opposite of believing the facts—a blind leap into fantasy. Their ridicule is misplaced—the living God and Jesus Christ his Son, are faithful and trustworthy. Jesus' life, death, and resurrection are open to scrutiny in the biblical records of eye-witnesses and their close associates.

Jesus has dealt fully with the great rift at the back of the fear of eternity. Now, through trust in him we receive the gift of peace with God on the basis of his Son's intervention in this world.

This chapter has delved into atheism, which many assume to be based on science, and that belief in Jesus is merely a leap without evidence. I have explained that nothing could be further from the truth.

Now, with an open Bible, we know why fears are real and a lot more than complex chemistry. We now know our humanity has real trouble and real fear. We already knew God existed, but didn't want to know.

Atheism is not a rational answer for why everything is as it is, for it throws away the key to unlock reality. For an atheist, to be trapped by the thought that, on its own terms, atheistic beliefs are meaningless, creates hopeless anger that assaults their humanity.

> We already knew God existed, but didn't want to know

Atheists face the challenge of eternity

Jesus Christ, who has revealed the living creator God, is the final answer to the terrible darkness. Jesus is called *the Word*, who *was in the beginning with God* (John 1:2). He is the personal origin of conscious persons and true communication—and he is deity—*the Word was God* (John 1:1). He is also the creator, for *all things were made through him, and without him was not any thing made that was made* (John 1:3). Trusting in Jesus is never a leap, but a confident reliance on his utterly dependable person.

Chapter 7

Jesus said, speaking about the living God: *whoever sees me sees him who sent me. I have come into the world as light, so that whoever believes in me may not remain in darkness* (John 12:45–46). Now you have no excuse.

What a choice—the darkness of atheism, or the light of Christ!

Atheists too face the challenge of eternity. It's time to face reality.

8. God—time and eternity

God is infinitely greater than we think. He dwarfs our tiny thoughts. The living God is *majestic in holiness, awesome in glorious deeds, doing wonders* (Exodus 15:11). God is flawless, not marred by the slightest imperfection. In all his abilities, he is perfect, beyond our little grasp—*Out of Zion, the perfection of beauty, God shines forth* (Psalm 50:2). God knows all things and is infinite in love, justice, wisdom and power. He is perfect beyond our comprehension. Have you ever bowed your head in the presence of his awesome majesty? This is the living God from whom Jesus came in his deity and humanity to live among us.

Everlasting

God is beyond time and our thoughts of eternity. He is the one, *who alone has immortality, who dwells in unapproachable light* (1 Timothy 6:16). He created all things, and *before the mountains were brought forth, or ever you had formed the earth and the world, from everlasting to everlasting you are God* (Psalm 90:2). These words about immortality and everlasting show us that God is not limited by our understanding of time.

> God is not limited by our understanding of time

Rather, he created this whole vast physical reality immersed in what we call 'time', while the biblical words translated 'eternal', 'eternity', or 'everlasting' have the thoughts of 'enduring', 'unending', or belonging to 'the age to come'.

Some of the fear-stirring thoughts that fill people's minds come from how they think of a vast eternity of time, and the thought of being trapped in a prison of infinite time that keeps rolling on for ever. Oh, be careful what you think!

If you kept driving your car over the same stretch of soft ground, the tyres would soon form deep tracks. Some fears are like that. Once your thoughts have been there a few times, they begin to run in the same track and form a habit, which is then challenging to change.

Some of these unhelpful patterns of thought may become deep-seated, and need to be confronted with gentle perseverance, especially as we learn new truths from God's word.

So, in the Bible, eternity includes endlessness, but not as an abstract idea. It is much more that God, who *is spirit* (John 4:24), in his infinite glory, says of himself: *I AM WHO I AM* (Exodus 3:14). He only is the ever-existing origin of all reality and personal being.

In his exalted glory, God says an astonishing thing about himself: *For thus says the One who is high and lifted up, who inhabits eternity, whose name is Holy: 'I dwell in the high and holy place, and also with him who is of a contrite and lowly spirit'* (Isaiah 57:15). God is pleased to come right down to share his life with those who humble themselves before him.

Eternity

Why ever do we think about eternity in the first place? God's word has the answer: *He [God] has made everything beautiful in its time. Also, he has put eternity into man's heart* (Ecclesiastes 3:11).

We were made to appreciate the concept of eternity

These words show that we were made to appreciate the concept of eternity, even though we can only ever see 'eternity' with finite minds.

Also, from these truths we see that God exists beyond time and space in eternity, but that he comes down to live with people in time and space.

Jesus demonstrated this when he came from the highest place down into this world. He said he had *descended from heaven* (John 3:13), but then, when he was here, he welcomed people, saying, *Come to me, all who labour and are heavy laden, and I will give you rest* (Matthew 11:28).

There is nothing fear-filled minds need more than to find the rest Jesus offers and to trust his promise of peace. He understands how fragile we are. So, whatever your own difficulties, perhaps you have begun to see that mixed with various fears is a growing guilty fear of God's judgement, and that, above all else, your most urgent and vital need is to be *reconciled to God by the death of his Son* (Romans 5:10).

Even the unnerving fear of eternity, or other troubling fears, can at times mask our greatest need. So, as you consider Jesus' teaching about eternity, consider how the good news of his death and the offer of his true heart-rest is the final answer for your fear of God's judgement.

Even the pace of life is so often filled with stress and agitation that to find a place of stillness and quiet to let our minds slow down can be such a help. Find a place where you feel at ease to reflect on God's word, and pray that he will show you his help and his way.

Life

Perhaps you have heard the biblical words 'eternal life' but find the idea very unattractive. Jesus' use of the words is often quoted in John's Gospel, where for example we see he was emphatic: *Truly, truly, I say to you, whoever hears my word and believes him who sent me has eternal life. He does not come into judgement, but has passed from death to life* (John 5:24).

Just what does 'eternal life' mean in Jesus' teaching? For a start, even though endless duration is included, the emphasis is far more on the promise of a foretaste given in the present of a future fullness of life, a life ever fresh in the presence of God in the new eternal age to come.

This new life is given to the spiritually lifeless; it is a life given by God the Holy Spirit, which in its final future is full, rich and overflowing forever.

This is nothing like a disembodied existence of hopeless wandering for ever through infinite caverns of darkness; it is life in new, resurrected bodies such as Jesus had after his resurrection.

Possession

Jesus also said, *For this is the will of my Father, that everyone who looks to the Son and believes in him should have eternal life, and I will raise him up on the last day* (John 6:40). Eternal life is the gift of God, received by all who look to the Lord Jesus and who trust in him.

As a present possession, eternal life looks to a resurrected completion and a perfect wholeness in new bodies, that Jesus says he will accomplish at one very definite time—the last day. That day is the great Day of final Judgement, from which those who have received eternal life are already free from all condemnation. That is because the sacrifice of Jesus' death and his resurrection are the secure basis for the gift of eternal life.

> The sacrifice of Jesus' death and his resurrection are the secure basis for the gift of eternal life

We will look more fully at these vital truths later. For now we must face some bad news, but followed by wonderful good news: *the wages of sin is death, but the free gift of God is eternal life in Christ Jesus our Lord* (Romans 6:23). Is it time you asked God for this precious gift? This is the gift that causes all condemning fears to give up their hold, as now, *since we have been justified by faith, we have peace with God through our Lord Jesus Christ* (Romans 5:1). By trusting God's faithful and dependable promise, we are accepted and secure.

Some of the dark fears about 'eternal life' come from thinking that it is merely existing in an endless future, like this present life multiplied to become a hopeless, eternal prison without any vital God-filled content of love, peace and joy. Are you like that, still trying to escape from the challenge of eternity by shutting God out of your thoughts?

Near

Some have a religious hope of life forever in God's presence, without ever having received eternal life. Such hopes often rest on the sinking sands of religious rituals, good works, or the belief, 'I've never harmed anyone.' Don't bank on such empty hopes of gaining eternal life.

Three further vital truths come from the Apostle Paul's address to a group of Greek philosophers. To these deep thinkers Paul was clear that all people, wherever they live, *should seek God, and perhaps feel their way toward him and find him. Yet he is actually not far from each of us, for 'In him we live and move and have our being'* (Acts 17:27–28).

The final quote is likely from Epimenides, a philosopher from Crete, whom the Apostle quoted with approval to show which of their own thinkers' ideas contained a kernel of truth.

Find

The three great truths are:

1. That we should all seek to find God, and make that our urgent supreme search, until we find him—for God is accessible.

2. He is not a God far away, beyond the outer fringes of the cosmos, but is near at hand, far closer that we realise.

3. Even our own personal being and existence come from God. We exist within his all-pervading presence.

One of the wonders of God's grace towards wanderers like us is that he sent his own Son—*the only God, who is at the Father's side, he has made him known* (John 1:18). The word about having made him known means 'declared'. Jesus has openly and fully revealed God.

In Christ, the attributes of deity and humanity are in perfect union in one fully human and divine person. Infinity has entered time—the Eternal has come to live in our humanity. Jesus knows about our frailties and weaknesses and understands us.

Instead of those awful, mind-reeling thoughts that crash the gears of our logical reasoning, we are presented with a Christ in whom *the whole fullness of deity dwells bodily* (Colossians 2:9).

Now, the person who trusts in Christ is complete—*you have been filled in him* (Colossians 2:10). Christ, in all his fullness, is the source of the Christian's complete sufficiency. Eternal life is life with Christ, which begins in the present and continues with him in his eternal glory.

> Eternal life is life with Christ, which begins in the present and continues with him in his eternal glory

Personal

Do you see where this leads? Instead of the terrifying, endless dark mystery, we have a God-man, who in his divine fullness is able to fill that fearful void.

God is not a theoretical idea; he is a perfect unity of three co-equal and co-eternal persons—Father, Son, and Holy Spirit.

Today, the good news is that God has made the way to welcome all who will come to him confessing their sin and asking for his forgiveness. God's forgiveness is free and undeserved, but secured at such a cost on the cross, when Jesus endured the full penalty of sin on behalf of all who will trust him for the gift of peace with God.

Eternal life is a living relationship with God our Father, through his Son; a precious relationship that will never end.

9. Self-esteem—battle with fear

'Well'—you might say, 'That all sounds fine, but not so fast! My humanistic beliefs about self-esteem have helped me look positively at my fears—even if I haven't yet come to terms with eternity. So, if Jesus has an answer, what happens to my self-esteem?'

Adrift

Self-esteem is a hot topic in today's world. 'Western culture has come to view low self-esteem as the root of our every emotional problem, holding us back in life.'[12] How you build self-esteem in today's secular world is considered vital to how you survive and succeed.

If the new secular belief is a strong confidence in 'self', including self-esteem, self-fulfilment and self-promotion, how did we get here, and what is the belief system supporting self-esteem? We have already looked at how God's word reveals that after the entrance of sin, anxiety and fear have, in various ways, come to us all. Cut off from God, with a nature hostile to him, people everywhere still look for answers. They look for meaning and how to cope with their anxious uncertainties and fears.

Today, the main way to do this is to build self-esteem. But on what foundation will you build, and does it succeed in the battle with fear?

> On what foundation will you build, and does it succeed in the battle with fear?

The secular view of 'self' often refers to a collection of drives and needs at the centre of each person. Before the term 'self-esteem' became popular, other expressions such as 'self-actualisation', 'self-respect', and 'self-worth', 'self-confidence' and 'self-understanding' all played a part, and still do.

---

12 Michael Reeves, *Rejoice & Tremble—the surprising good news of the Fear of the Lord* (Crossway, Wheaton, Illinois), 2021, p. 141.

Psychology

With the rise of popular secular psychology in the late nineteenth century, a number of key thinkers developed various approaches to life's questions. Some of their names are still well-known: Sigmund Freud, Carl Jung, Erich Fromm, Abraham Maslow and Carl Rogers were intrigued by subjects like: personality, mind, motivation, guilt, meaning, and psychological wholeness.

A lot of this thinking held that humanity was essentially good. But some of it believed that despite a lot of positive traits, there was an inherent evil behind aggression, war, broken relationships and fear. Over time, various schools of thought attracted wide followings hoping to reach the goal of psychological wholeness.

Against this background, the modern secular belief in personal self-esteem aims to raise an individual's sense of self-value and self-appreciation into a positive self-image.

Add to this goal the need to feel good, and today the popular way is to follow the heart. If something feels good, that is the way to go.

Goals

Of course, at times there is a sharp conflict between aggressive feelings towards a person and the need to respond in a socially acceptable way. Some people may then feel self-doubt or guilt and a loss of confidence and become fearful of consequences.

Life is complex, and efforts to build self-esteem struggle with many issues, not least with fear. As to the deeper meaning of life and coping with real adversity, trouble and fear, secular self-esteem has no answers of sure and certain hope, or for those nagging fears about eternity.

> Secular self-esteem has no answers of sure and certain hope, or for those nagging fears about eternity

We noted this in our appraisals of evolution and atheism. Exclude the living God and all that Jesus taught and accomplished, and there is no meaning to life. Modern psychology is not the final answer. Secular labelling of personal difficulties as if it was an illness is confusing—'Problems of living are NOT mental illnesses!' [13]

Value

But, you may ask, is it that wrong to be self-centred, when the Bible teaches us to be concerned about our own relationship with God?

What's the difference between popular self-esteem beliefs and the teaching of Jesus? After all, God commands: *you shall love your neighbour as yourself* (Leviticus 19:18), calling not for a self-absorbed concern, but a healthy self-love.

Jesus quoted those words, placing them after the first and great commandment, when he said, *And you shall love the Lord your God with all your heart and with all your soul and with all your mind and with all your strength. The second is this; you shall love your neighbour as yourself* (Mark 12:30–31). Remember, love is not a feeling, but a commitment.

Love is not a feeling, but a commitment

If there is a genuine self-love, as those words teach, a love that includes our care and concern for our health, education, protection and our eternal interest, how do we separate that from self-esteem beliefs? From some of the biblical examples we have given of how people who suffered real adversity and fears were helped by God's word, was that also their way of raising their self-esteem? The straight answer is 'no', because they did not set out with that goal, but rather to turn to God for his help because he was worthy of their trust.

They became confident, not in themselves but in God whose word helped them in their trial. Their insight was God-centred—a very different goal from that of secular self-esteem.

---

13 Martin and Deidre Bobgan, *Psychoheresy—The Psychological Seduction of Christianity* (Eastgate Publishers, California, 1987), p. 138.

Chapter 9

Love

However, the command to love others as we love ourselves is a serious challenge, but given in the context of a God-centred life in which, first of all, the very goal of our being is to love him supremely. In sharp contrast, secular self-esteem belief excludes God and instead puts our self-love first. No wonder people lose in the battle with fear!

Michael Reeves has looked closely at this, and concludes: '...the cure doesn't work. Seeking to bolster our self-esteem by making us ... *more self-conscious* is only making us more vulnerable and thin-skinned.'[14] The drive of self-esteem to build a secure identity is like building on sand. Many become over-absorbed with their new self-made identity.

Then, instead of growing in confidence, it fills them with anxious insecurity, never quite sure of what their identity is, but fearful of getting hurt and damaged. The cure they hoped to find failed them.

> Jesus' teaching reveals the one way to face our fears and to find a new identity in him

Despite the powerful secular consensus, this is not the way to true peace. These beliefs, so popular today, fail in the light of Jesus' teaching, where self-esteem has no future in self-created identities. Instead, we find Jesus' teaching reveals the one way to face our fears and to find a new identity in him.

He had some heart-searching things to say. Just as the first and great command is an all or nothing matter in relation to the love of God, so is Jesus' teaching about himself. His hearers were not slow to see Jesus' meaning, which aroused strong hostility—*he was even calling God his own Father, making himself equal with God* (John 5:18).

Jesus claimed a perfect obedience in his filial relationship with God and an exclusive knowledge of God's personal activity—*For whatever the Father does, that the Son does likewise. For the Father loves the Son and shows him all that he himself is doing* (John 5:19–20).

---

14 Michael Reeves, *Rejoice & Tremble*, p. 141.

Describing this mission, Jesus said: *For I have come down from heaven, not to do my own will but the will of him who sent me* (John 6:38). Jesus lived out this exalted claim to have come in person from heaven on a clearly defined mission to do his Father's will.

Die!

When Jesus called people to turn and follow him, we see the same all or nothing challenge—*If anyone would come after me, let him deny himself and take up his cross and follow me. For whoever would save his life will lose it, but whoever loses his life for my sake and the gospel's will save it. For what does it profit a man to gain the whole world and forfeit his soul? For what can a man give in return for his soul?* (Mark 8:34–37).

In those searching words we face Jesus' call to die to self-centred ambition and follow him with wholehearted loving devotion. This is a giving up of all self-centred plans of worldly success, personal vanity and pride—trying to save one's life the way the world views success, by gaining wealth, recognition and admiring followers. Is that life?

No, Jesus says that is the way to empty souls and fearful loss.

Life

But for those who are willing to lose all that this world has to offer and give their lives to Jesus Christ and the gospel, they will find true life. For, even if one could gain all the prestige, wealth and glory of this quickly-passing world at the cost of the eternal loss of their soul, there is no comparison.

This entire world's wealth is no bargaining chip with God and utterly useless to save one's ever-living soul—and no way to face the challenge of eternity.

Jesus' call to weigh up all and then follow him is enabled by the gift of a new life from God. He made this an absolute necessity, when he said to a leading religious teacher, *You must be born again. The wind blows where it wishes, and you hear its sound, but you do not know where it comes from or where it goes. So it is with everyone who is born of the Spirit* (John 3:7–8). There are no half measures in Jesus' words—'you must…' Ignore this and you miss life itself; a life given by God's Holy Spirit.

Then, when we see how this new life is lived out in practice after Jesus' death and resurrection, we find the same truths explained in the gospel and how the Lord Jesus still calls for a total commitment to him.

Total

Take the Apostle Paul, for example. He had been a proud, intellectual young Pharisee, quickly rising in influence among his peers. He then compares all that with what he had received freely in Christ: *But whatever gain I had, I counted as loss for the sake of Christ. Indeed, I count everything as loss because of the surpassing worth of knowing Christ Jesus my Lord. For his sake I have suffered the loss of all things and count them as rubbish, in order that I may gain Christ* (Philippians 3:7–8).

When Paul weighed it all up, his loss was refuse compared with all he had gained in Christ and received as a gift, even a perfect-standing with God. This was nothing less than Christ's own position of acceptance credited to Paul. So, he finished up, *not having a righteousness of my own that comes from the law, but that which comes through faith in Christ, the righteousness from God that depends on faith* (Philippians 3:9), where, in those words, 'faith' means personal trust.

Gain

No greater gain is possible. This is where worldly ambitions pale to rubbish compared with the love of Christ and God's welcome into his family.

Paul then sounds the death knell to self-esteem when he explains what the identification with Jesus in his death means for everyone who receives God's way of getting right with him. He says: *I have been crucified with Christ. It is no longer I who live, but Christ who lives in me. And the life I now live in the flesh I live by faith in the Son of God, who loved me and gave himself for me. I do not nullify the grace of God, for if righteousness were through the law, then Christ died for no purpose* (Galatians 2:20–21).

There is a lot packed into those words—here is a summary:

In that magnificent statement we find that the Christian life is all about what Jesus accomplished by his death. On the cross, he offered himself as the substitute for everyone who will trust in him, so that each believer is then freely credited with all that Christ accomplished on their behalf. Identification with Jesus in his death changes everything.

Identification with Jesus in his death changes everything

Paul is speaking for each person who trusts in Christ. When we do that, confessing our sins to God, trusting that Christ died in our place, our sinful, condemned 'I' has already been crucified with Christ.

My substitute

My old sinful self inherited from Adam, including my proud, foolish efforts to build self-esteem, died with Christ. God judged all that I was as a sinner in Christ my substitute, who died the death I deserved and so brought my old relationship to what I once was in Adam to an end.

Being crucified with Christ is a once-for-all event, completed for ever, but one on which I continue to reckon each day as I live Christ's way, where the open secret is—it is not death to die. God's Holy Spirit now shares Christ's indwelling presence and, by his enabling, now I live day by day trusting in Christ, the one who, loving me, even gave himself for me. With God's love all my need for false self-esteem vanishes.

Law and love

Rather than crushing my personality, God gives me the fullest life in spiritual union with Christ

Rather than crushing my personality, God gives me the fullest life in spiritual union with Christ. Now, I reject my fickle feelings and live by trusting God's faithful word, which reveals that Jesus kept God's law perfectly on my behalf, and then died a death in which he endured the penalty I deserved as a divine law-breaker.

Paul then clinches his case. If I could have attained a right-standing with God by all my efforts at keeping God's law of commandments, Jesus' death would have been completely unnecessary. But, instead of that, Paul is overwhelmed by the personal love of the Son of God. For now, not only for Paul, but to all who trust in Christ crucified and risen, his own spotless right-standing with God is credited to each as *the free gift of righteousness* (Romans 5:17)—and the case is settled.

Self-esteem can never give life or succeed in the battle with fear. But in Christ, what a difference!—*we rejoice in hope of the glory of God. Not only that, but we rejoice in our sufferings, knowing that suffering produces endurance, and endurance produces character, and character produces hope, and hope does not put us to shame, because God's love has been poured into our hearts through the Holy Spirit who has been given to us* (Romans 5:2–5).

Resources

With such resources, even in times of great difficulty, God rescues us from fear—*I called on your name, O LORD, from the depths of the pit; you heard my plea, 'Do not close your ear to my cry for help!' You came near when I called on you; you said, 'Do not fear!'* (Lamentations 3:55–57).

So, if self-esteem beliefs have no answer for fear as they exclude God and focus on your feelings and self, it is time to reckon that dying to self through personal trust in Jesus Christ is life. With your focus on Christ you have his resources to overcome your old self-focused fears.

10. Jesus and eternal life

Some people still protest—'It's not right to worry people about eternity!' Even so, many are already worried by it, and evading it helps no one. Often the fear of eternity is linked to the fear of death. So, if you still have nagging fears about it, this is the time to consider how Jesus' death has dealt with those fears, and how he gives eternal life.

Eternity and Jesus

Speaking of himself, Jesus said, *No one has ascended into heaven except he who descended from heaven, the Son of Man* (John 3:13). He came into our world as the Lord of all, divine yet truly human, with no sin of his own, to put himself in the place of others and die for their sins. God then accepted Jesus' sacrifice and raised him on the third day, when he *was declared to be the Son of God in power according to the Spirit of holiness by his resurrection from the dead, Jesus Christ our Lord* (Romans 1:4). Several weeks later he ascended back to God his Father.

Then, at the end of time, we shall all be called to give an account to him as the Judge of all. Many are anxious about this, and with good reason.

However, this is not an issue for secular counselling. Jesus came to resolve all such fear. But, first we need to know that he who is love, who made the blind to see, the lame to walk, children to sing, who forgave sins, also gave the direst warnings about eternal punishment.

> If love warns about danger, infinite love must warn about infinite danger

So, if love warns about danger, infinite love must warn about infinite danger. Thus, Jesus warned that those who reject him will go *into the eternal fire prepared for the devil and his angels. He also said: these will go away into eternal punishment* (Matthew 25:41 and 25:46). Just as Jesus spoke about eternal life, he also spoke about eternal punishment.

Sin is infinitely serious

His mission was to pay love's supreme price in death to rescue people from that most terrible end. He made it very clear: *For God so loved the world, that he gave his only Son, that whoever believes in him should not perish but have eternal life* (John 3:16). That is love like no other.

Sin is serious beyond measure—it is the defiant rejection of Almighty God and his moral standard; *sin is lawlessness* (1 John 3:4). But by nature we are all *dead in the trespasses and sins* (Ephesians 2:1), in which we have lived. This cuts us off from God's favour, and leaves us spiritually dead, and under his condemnation.

The Bible describes our condition as *alienated from the life of God* (Ephesians 4:18), and as *children of wrath* (Ephesians 2:3), deserving God's judgement of eternal punishment. No one is served by thinking their problem is less serious than it actually is. We need to accept what God says about our condition and then take steps to deal with it.

> No one is served by thinking their problem is less serious than it actually is

Jesus' words, *'eternal punishment'* (Matthew 25:46) refer to God's judgement at the end of this present age of all who have finally rejected Christ; a just punishment from which there is no escape—ever. This is the backdrop against which the gospel of Christ continues to be such wonderful good news.

In making an escape so that people would *not perish* (John 3:16), by an action of infinite love suffering infinite loss, this is not less than an astonishing rescue that the Son of God undertook in his death.

No other good news will ever outclass it. These are ultimate issues, and warning people compassionately of *the wrath to come* (Luke 3:7) is meant to help them see the greatness of God's love in making an eternal escape from his wrath. God did that once in Jesus' death, when he carried sin's condemnation on behalf of all those who would confess that they deserved such judgement themselves, but then trust that Jesus had carried it all for them. God's wrath is his perfectly measured, holy anger against anything that rejects his perfect standard and his way of salvation; but it is never a fitful display of uncontrolled rage.

Eternal

Despite the clear biblical truth of eternal punishment, some have a false hope that God will merely annihilate all those who have not received eternal life in Christ. This is often called 'conditional immortality' because immortality—living for ever—is conditional on personal faith in Christ. Those who believe this are hoping that all who fail to meet that condition of personal faith are annihilated, either at death, or on Judgement Day. Many non-Christians already have this false hope, which reduces their persons from divine image-bearers to mere animals. They overlook that, *it is appointed for man to die once, and after that comes judgement* (Hebrews 9:27). Clearly then, judgement follows *after* physical death.

The false idea assumes that as only God is immortal his gift of eternal life and immortality is given only to those who receive it, while those who reject it are annihilated on Judgement Day. Never rely on either of these false ways of escaping from your anxiety about God's judgement.

Immortal

God *alone has immortality* (1 Timothy 6:16) but he gives a perfect and glorious eternal life in heaven to all who receive this gift of God who, in Christ, *abolished death and brought life and immortality to light through the gospel* (2 Timothy 1:10). However, all those who are already spiritually dead in sin, and who refuse to repent, still have an eternal soul and remain under God's judgement, even after death.

They are subject to death in its most final sense, which is to be eternally and consciously separated from God. That is what Jesus' words about eternal punishment refer to. But 'conditional immortality' rejects Christ's clear words of eternal punishment and prefers to hold out for extinction, which some call 'annihilation'.

These beliefs are not the answer for the way to peace with God. If those who die as rebels against God do not suffer eternally but are only annihilated, why did Christ suffer being cut off and judged by God his Father? (See Matthew 27:46.) Mere annihilation would not require this, but would change the goal of Jesus' death. Annihilation is not a trivial little piece of false optimism. Far from it, the Bible is very clear that all those who finally reject the offer of eternal life in Christ and who refuse to repent, continue after death to be unique personal beings. They remain for ever as God's personal image-bearers banished to remain under his holy condemnation that is their just due.

God is just and loving

As well as Jesus' words of loving and tender entreaty, he repeatedly warned his hearers in the most solemn words. He spoke about a great separation at the end of time, when those who had caused others to sin and *all law-breakers* would be thrown *into the fiery furnace*. He spoke about some being cast into *outer darkness. In that place there will be weeping and gnashing of teeth* (Matthew 13:41–42 and 22:13). Jesus spoke about this place as hell, where *the fire is not quenched* (Mark 9:48).

He was emphatic: *an hour is coming when all who are in the tombs will hear his voice* [that is, his own voice] *and come out, those who have done good to the resurrection of life, and those who have done evil to the resurrection of judgement* (John 5:28–29). In summary, and this is vital, *there will be a resurrection of both the just and the unjust* (Acts 24:15).

But the 'conditional immortality' belief shrinks the goal of Jesus' death to one in which he saves sinners for heaven, but only from non-existence; a very different salvation from that revealed in God's word.

A great salvation

There, the central glory of the eternal ages is that God's own Son accomplished a salvation so vast that he suffered a condemnation more than sufficient to save countless numbers from eternal punishment.

In a future time a new song of amazed thanks will be sung to the Son of God—*for you were slain, and by your blood you ransomed people for God from every tribe and language and people and nation* (Revelation 5:9). That leaves one conclusion: Jesus paid that full, most terrible price.

Nothing else but Jesus' death, which *God put forward as a propitiation by his blood, to be received by faith* (Romans 3:25) saved sinners from *eternal punishment* (Matthew 25:46). Propitiation means that Jesus suffered the wrath of God on behalf of sinners to fully pacify and quench his just, holy anger that would otherwise have justly sent all sinners to an eternal punishment. He did that in overflowing grace and mercy so as to save, with a breath-taking salvation, all who trust in his saving work. Jesus paid it all—*you were bought with a price* (1 Corinthians 6:20)—a very great price!

No condemnation

This point is vital: God's Son did not die merely to save people from annihilation. He died to rescue all who will turn and trust him—past, present and future, from God's just sentence of eternal punishment.

> God's Son did not die merely to save people from annihilation

Jesus' words ring out: *Whoever believes in the Son has eternal life; whoever does not obey the Son shall not see life, but the wrath of God remains on him* (John 3:36). His words bring you the personal challenge of eternity.

But don't think of eternal life as only far off in the distant future; it is a present relationship with God through Jesus Christ, who in prayer to his Father said, *And this is eternal life, that they know you the only true God, and Jesus Christ whom you have sent* (John 17:3).

So, come and leave your anxious fears about eternity and death with him, and receive peace with God through a personal reliance on Christ. For all who repent and trust that Jesus took their place in his death, his blood secured *an eternal redemption* (Hebrews 9:12). He paid the supreme price to secure their rescue, so that all who obey his call *may receive the promised eternal inheritance* (Hebrews 9:15). What peace, knowing that Jesus' death has dealt the death blow to the fear of death!

Ready

In the first few centuries of the Christian Church, there were periods when organised persecution of Christians was intense. But rather than pay homage to Caesar as a god, many Christians gave their lives to wild beasts for the thrill of packed Roman arenas.

In more recent centuries of great hostility, many Christians chose to be martyred and burnt at the stake, rather than deny their precious Saviour. Throughout history, to the present day, Christian men and women, and children, have breathed their last in the calm assurance that the Lord Jesus had come to take them home to be with him. They had the wonderful certainty that as Jesus had come once to die for their sins, so their joy then, in the words of the Apostle Paul, was to *be with Christ, for that is far better* (Philippians 1:23).

One further truth concerns the bodily resurrection of God's children, who will be given new transformed bodies like Jesus had when he was raised from the tomb.

Between the time of the *putting off* (2 Peter 1:14) of our body in death, and the second coming of the Lord, the spirits of God's children will be *with Christ* (Philippians 1:23), ready for the day of resurrection.

We are not going to live as wandering, disembodied spirits. All who belong to Christ will receive perfect personal and bodily unity when the Lord *will transform our lowly body to be like his glorious body* (Philippians 3:21). This transformation fits us for life in God's new creation—his *new heavens and a new earth in which righteousness dwells* (2 Peter 3:13). Fears dissolve in the light of this reassuring truth of God's purpose in salvation and new creation through Christ.

Today

The worst thing troubled people can do is to try and desensitise their fears by alcohol, sedatives or humanistic solutions. Never try to quash an uneasy conscience or fight even the gentle conviction of sin, which is meant to stir you to turn away from your sins and trust in Christ. Instead, will you accept this strong, loving appeal: *We implore you on behalf of Christ, be reconciled to God* (2 Corinthians 5:20)? Never keep on putting off what you know you must do, for *now is the favourable time; behold, now is the day of salvation* (2 Corinthians 6:2).

The Lord Jesus is fully trustworthy. Trust him today and be assured—*I write these things to you who believe in the name of the Son of God that you may know that you have eternal life* (1 John 5:13). The 'belief' mentioned here refers to a restful trust in the person of the Lord Jesus, by which you know for sure that you have received eternal life as the gift of God. For those who once knew deep guilt, what powerful words of peace!

Rest your uncertainties with him. No one else but Jesus will get you through the challenge of eternity!

Precious promise

Jesus' own death has dealt with the terrors of death—for he endured them himself, fully and finally for all those who receive God's gift of eternal life. He said, *I am the resurrection and the life. Whoever believes in me, though he die, yet shall he live, and everyone who lives and believes in me shall never die* (John 11:25–26).

> Jesus' own death has dealt with the terrors of death—for he endured them himself, fully and finally for all those who receive God's gift of eternal life

Will you trust Jesus' words in that precious promise, and then live in the light of them?

The final two chapters will help you to do that.

11. The mind of Christ

By now we have seen that fears such as those arising from moral guilt, and the fear of eternity and death have been resolved by Jesus' death. They are fully settled forever for all who have trusted in Jesus and what he has done for them. The challenge of eternity is settled.

Life

We have also seen that through personal trust in Christ we begin a new life in which the mind plays a vital role. For now, instead of our thoughts and fears bearing down on us like a fearful avalanche of destruction, completely out of control, we are given new resources of self-control to face the challenges and guide our thinking.

> We are given new resources of self-control to face the challenges and guide our thinking

Our thinking is no longer a wild untameable tyrant, but called to submit in love to the will of God. This is revolutionary. This is life. This is the subject of discovering and following *the mind of Christ* (1 Corinthians 2:16).

Press on

This subject will help you to see that if you have trusted in Christ, you will persevere through trials, which will assure you God has begun a life-transforming work in you. In all these trials we begin to see the way God uses them to mould us, as we now know that we were saved for good works, but never by them.

Slowly (it seems) you learn to look more and more to Jesus Christ, your Lord and Saviour. You begin to see that instead of self-focused thoughts, you become more Christ-focused—and more God-centred. This is the mind of Christ.

In all this, whether in times of quiet or facing trials, God's word calls for our minds to be transformed by God the Holy Spirit. Here we are challenged by the command to *love the Lord your God with all your heart and with all your soul and with all your mind and with all your strength* (Mark 12:30). In light of Jesus' love, this is to be our glad response.

The word 'all' is repeated four times and applied to every part of our person; our 'heart', 'soul', 'mind', and 'strength'. Nothing is left out, so that we might be persons fully complete in our love of God—for *'What no eye has seen, nor ear heard, nor the heart of man imagined, what God has prepared for those who love him'—these things God has revealed to us through the Spirit* (1 Corinthians 2:9–10). What glorious truths God has already revealed to his children!

> God's word calls for our minds to be transformed by God the Holy Spirit

Calling

There is something majestic about this high and holy calling in its completeness, because its object is God himself. He is to be our supreme pursuit, our entire delight, our glory.

These are big challenges, but in the riches of biblical Christianity and its application to the minds and lives of God's children, there is no space left for unworthy thoughts. Nor space for trivial distractions such as distorted, fearful thoughts about eternity.

To make this clear let's briefly look at five key biblical truths that relate directly to the mind. In list form, these are:

1. 1 Corinthians 2:16—we have the mind of Christ.

2. Romans 8:5-6—the wrong and the right focus of the mind.

3. Romans 12:2—the transformed mind.

4. 2 Timothy 1:7—a sound mind—whole, healthy and courageous.

5. Philippians 2:5-8—let this mind be in you.

Character

As this subject is so vital, we must note what the mind of Christ does not mean for our Christian life. It is not a sort of sinless perfection in all of our thinking, neither is it a sort of supernatural transplant of Christ's mind into our own, nor is it a once-for-all experience. Finally, it is not a state of super-spirituality that gives me the idea that I am able to look down on other Christians as less than myself.

There is a lot that the mind of Christ in us does not mean. Keep them in mind! If that is what our subject does not mean, we had better look at the five Bible truths about what it does mean.

1. In this first point we note that the Apostle Paul encouraged the Christians at Corinth by sharing that all who were in spiritual union with Christ had received wisdom from God. If you have trusted in Christ you too have received God's wisdom revealed in the meaning of Jesus' death. You have been taught by God the Holy Spirit—no small honour! Then Paul asks, *who has understood the mind of the Lord so as to instruct him? But we have the mind of Christ* (1 Corinthians 2:16).

What is Paul getting at? He is not talking about himself as an especially inspired Apostle, but about the spiritual position of all believers in Christ. That is why he says 'we have the mind of Christ'. When Paul brought the good news to Corinth, those who trusted in Christ had accepted not natural, human wisdom, as our foolish attempt to tell God how he should think, like the secular Greek thinkers. Instead, the Christians had accepted God's own wisdom that he had taught them.

> The Christians had accepted God's own wisdom that he had taught them

Loved beyond value

They had learned to value the wonderful truths of a full and free salvation, accomplished by Jesus once for all in his death on the cross. This is the sense, then, in which we have the mind of Christ, as it expresses the wisdom of God. Of course, this is never a complete or perfect wisdom, but a true and precious divine wisdom nevertheless.

The reality is that if you have turned from your own secular thinking and false beliefs, and trusted in the Lord Jesus Christ as your sin-bearer and ever-living Saviour, you know you are loved beyond value, and have found rich treasures of spiritual wisdom in Christ. You accepted these truths *not as the word of men but as what it really is, the word of God, which is at work in you believers* (1 Thessalonians 2:13).

2. Then these words from Romans challenge us on what to focus our minds: *For those who live according to the flesh set their minds on the things of the flesh, but those who live according to the Spirit set their minds on the things of the Spirit. For to set the mind on the flesh is death, but to set the mind on the Spirit is life and peace* (Romans 8:5–6).

A mind set on the flesh is controlled by sinful bodily appetites, which lead to it being consumed by self-centredness, jealousy, sinful ambitions, anger and fear. That is the way to death, in which a person lives who has not yet come to place their trust in Christ.

But for the person who belongs to Christ, he or she is in union with him and knows they have died to sin in Christ's death on their behalf.

Now, they know that *sin will have no dominion over you, since you are not under law but under grace* (Romans 6:14). God's law points out our failures and condemns us, but his grace, his undeserved favour, brings salvation that breaks the ruling power of sin in our lives.

In this new position the Christian focuses on not grieving the Holy Spirit, but on developing a fruit-bearing relationship with Christ. Such enjoy a life of purity, peace and joy. But even with the mind of Christ, we must make progress in our growth to maturity.

> In this new position the Christian focuses on not grieving the Holy Spirit, but on developing a fruit-bearing relationship with Christ

Chapter 11

Transformed

3. In developing a mind at one with Christ's own mind, we aim for a transformed mind—*Do not be conformed to this world, but be transformed by the renewal of your mind, that by testing you may discern what is the will of God, what is good and acceptable and perfect* (Romans 12:2).

God calls each Christian to turn away from the pressures of the popular ways of thinking in this fallen world. This is where we face all of its subtle, sinful rebellion against God, but instead of going with the flow, we aim to do the will of God. So, we turn away from the corrupting conformity and its evil pressures and gladly yield to the process of courageous change—a wonderful restoring and renewing of our minds, which God works in us, as his new creations in Christ.

God's purpose is to restore our minds to a pure, holy and healthy mind-set. This will involve our prayerful learning to choose the best way when faced with various options, as we learn to develop the precious faculty of a God-approved discernment. Such discernment will always be guided and taught by the word of God.

> God's purpose is to restore our minds to a pure, holy and healthy mind-set

The mind that is being transformed is on the pathway to developing the Spirit-controlled, humble, and loving mind of Christ.

4. Timothy helped the Apostle Paul in pastoral service in several young churches. But at times, Timothy felt out of his depth facing the many people-problems and needing to share clear teaching. He would have preferred a quieter, less challenging role in which to serve the Lord.

We briefly noted these words earlier, but now we must apply them.

Paul got to the centre of Timothy's problems with this reassurance: *For God gave us a spirit not of fear but of power and love and self-control* (2 Timothy 1:7). Those few words pack vital encouragement as we see that strong negative—God is not the source of our fears. Rather, by his Spirit, he has given us ample resources to support our minds in situations that seem far beyond us, even in circumstances that include threats from those who are hostile to the gospel.

Mission

Timidity is not an option; rule it out, and in its place develop an outgoing care that puts the interests of others before your own. For that we will need all three of the resources Paul mentions: power as the ability to act in the strength that God supplies, giving perseverance in hardship that resists timid retreat; then, self-giving, loving concern that serves the needs of others; finally, sound thinking and consistent self-control that accepts pressure, and rejects excitable, thoughtless impulses. This too is learning to develop the mind of Christ.

5. Finally, in Christ we have the supreme example of servanthood as a model for all Christians. Paul highlights this when he says, *Have this mind among yourselves, which is yours in Christ Jesus, who, though he was in the form of God, did not count equality with God a thing to be grasped, but emptied himself, by taking the form of a servant, being born in the likeness of men. And being found in human form, he humbled himself by becoming obedient to the point of death, even death on a cross* (Philippians 2:5–8).

When Jesus came in the veiled deity of the eternal Son of God, he came in lowliness on a mission to serve: first, in serving others, then by going to death itself, even that most degrading and humiliating form of death, invented for common criminals by barbaric Romans.

He did that in order to deal with sin and to open the door to eternal life for all who would receive God's gift. What a challenge for us, even as we aim to serve him, to develop the same attitude of serving others that was so conspicuous in Jesus himself!

God's word teaches us to have the same sort of thinking and motivation among ourselves, which is ours in Christ Jesus.

Wisdom

If that is where you are at, hold fast to all that God has given you, and give thanks that you have received such priceless treasure. Then grow in all that which is yours in Christ. Reject the appealing voice of feelings, and never believe what you feel if it contradicts God's word.

The following words are a prayer with a heart-searching challenge:

> *May the mind of Christ my Saviour*
> *live in me from day to day,*
> *by his love and power controlling*
> *all I do and say.*
>
> Kate B. Wilkinson (1859-1928).

12. Jesus Christ—eternal LOVE

We have looked at Jesus and eternity, as well as the fear of eternity and various other fears. Along the way, we aimed to expose some of the false hopes and refuges that people use to deal with their fears. Our goal was to place the origin of sinful fear in the Genesis fall, in our first parents' self-centred revolt against God. For that, God condemned them to alienation, psychological problems and death so that you could then see the amazing way God chose to provide the great reconciliation.

He did that through Jesus' death, when he suffered the penalty due to rebel sinners on their behalf, and brought reconciliation through his outpoured love on the cross; a love received in the gift of eternal life.

Problem solved

In dealing with various fears such as eternity, death and judgement, all were resolved by the death of Christ and by trust in him. God has made a way to restore lost sinners to his favour. Now the way back to God is open. Jesus *is able to save to the uttermost those who draw near to God through him* (Hebrews 7:25). He welcomes all.

No one is too bad or hopeless to receive his welcome. There was rich mercy, even for the angry, proud religious zealot, Saul from Tarsus, who had worked mercilessly to rid the world of Christianity. Based on the way the Lord had freely forgiven his sin and hostile campaign, Paul was able to share how, *The saying is trustworthy and deserving of full acceptance, that Christ Jesus came into the world to save sinners, of whom I am the foremost. But I received mercy* (1 Timothy 1:15–16).

> Faith is not the opposite of believing the facts. These great truths are grounded in credible historical events that invite reasoned thought and careful response

Faith is not the opposite of believing the facts. These great truths are grounded in credible historical events that invite reasoned thought and careful response. They never invite a leap into fictional fantasy, but rather call you to repent, confess and rest all your confidence in the faithful and dependable person of Jesus Christ.

So, we have urged you to look to the once crucified, now risen Saviour, who died for the sins of others. Look to Christ—he is the answer!

Make sure you trust him, who is able to save you for time and for eternity. God's grace is sufficient for whatever you will face, as you respond to his call and give yourself to his good purpose for your life.

Powerful gospel

We also see God's great purpose in one of the conclusions Paul draws in his letter to the Christians at Rome. This is nearly overwhelming, as the Apostle shows that the

> The child of God can never be separated from the love of Christ

child of God can never be separated from the love of Christ. He had unfolded how the good news of salvation in Christ is the outworking of God's eternal purpose. In this, *we know that for those who love God all things work together for good, for those who are called according to his purpose* (Romans 8:28).

God's purpose has an astonishing goal—for all who heard his call and trusted in Christ, were *predestined to be conformed to the image of his Son* (Romans 8:29). This goal is set to glorify the God of grace, for God, the supreme craftsman, already had this goal planned before creation, to restore countless fallen rebels to the moral beauty of Jesus.

Paul then goes on to explain how in this unfolding eternal purpose there is an unbreakable chain of God's actions. He says, *And those whom he predestined he also called, and those whom he called he also justified, and those whom he justified he also glorified* (Romans 8:30).

This powerful statement describes how God's purpose is accomplished through Christ. As the gospel of Christ is shared to great numbers of people, many hear the personal call of God. They repent of their sin and trust in the Lord Jesus for salvation. God's great promise in this was to forgive all their sins and declare them to be 'justified'—righteous in his sight, freely—wholly unmerited and undeserved.

Eternal purpose

With such a welcome into God's family, they are heirs to the promises of God concerning eternal life, in the present and the future. So, having been justified, they will then also certainly be glorified. On the golden morning of resurrection, when the Lord returns in universal splendour, each one of his family will be glorified and given a new body like that which Jesus was given when God raised him from the tomb.

This chain of God's unfolding purpose is given in his word to enlighten and encourage his children. God's unbreakable purpose in salvation is full of his grace. In this purpose, he works in each of his children, so that they overcome trials, temptations and the often severe difficulties that 'work together for good' in the training ground of this fallen world. God uses all these various challenges to transform their lives to become more like Jesus—for his character is the master pattern.

This is all a part of the four-link chain of the Romans 8:30 passage; predestined—called—justified—glorified. After sharing that summary of God's eternal purpose, Paul explains it in more detail.

He says, in view of God's purpose for each of his children, and in spite of however severe the obstacles and trials, *If God is for us, who can be against us?* (Romans 8:31). Seeing that God has already acted amazingly, in the most self-sacrificial way, even to the extent of giving up his own Son to death, then—*how will he not also with him graciously give us all things?* (Romans 8:32). With Christ, God also gives his children resources for the whole of life, so we abound with every God-given sufficiency.

More than conquerors

After all, God himself has justified us—declared us to be in right-standing with him. Whoever then shall condemn *God's elect* (Romans 8:33)? None, for Christ has himself died and been condemned by God on behalf of all those of whom Jesus said, *whoever comes to me I will never cast out* (John 6:37). So, come now, trust in Christ. For then we are assured that the Jesus who died was raised by God to his right hand of authority, where he *is interceding for us* (Romans 8:34).

In view of such astonishing divine acts, which have brought us such incredible privilege, nothing will ever come between us and the love of Christ. Whatever happens, even *tribulation* [serious trouble], *or distress, or persecution, or famine, or nakedness, or danger, or sword* (Romans 8:35), the believer is secure in Christ's love. In fact, *in all these things we are more than conquerors through him who loved us* (Romans 8:37).

Even though these are great difficulties, they do not bring us down, for through Christ we have his inexhaustible resources of love, endurance and power to overcome them, and become more than conquerors!

To the Christians at Corinth, Paul says he was once so overwhelmed by a vision of paradise that *he heard things that cannot be told, which man may not utter* (2 Corinthians 12:4).

How amazing! Paul heard secrets that were not part of God's special revelation for this world. But, now in his letter to the Christians at Rome, there is no such ban as God gives Paul a flow of exalted, passionate eloquence.

In it he ascends to a height nearly beyond words as he details a catalogue of events and conditions which, like the ultimate insurance policy, even if they were to occur, God's children are still covered. Whatever happens— whatever stands in the way—nothing will stop God from bringing his children to glory. Do not be afraid!

> Whatever happens— whatever stands in the way—nothing will stop God from bringing his children to glory. Do not be afraid!

He has already made the supreme action and pledged his promise. He has fully covered all eventualities, and not for one moment are his children ever out of his sight, or his love.

Ultimate assurance

Have no fear, these are the conditions, where not even, *death nor life, nor angels nor rulers, nor things present nor things to come, nor powers, nor height nor depth, nor anything else in all creation, will be able to separate us from the love of God in Christ Jesus our Lord* (Romans 8:38–39).

What great reassurance this gives that Paul was given full permission, on behalf of Almighty God, to confirm such generous certainty!

This is why Christ is all-sufficient and why God will never break the love bond that he has with his redeemed children. That is the challenge of ETERNITY—and why the answer is the love of Christ, from which nothing will ever separate those who belong to him.

That being the case, even today, come and cast all your anxieties on him. Then live for him as you *grow in the grace and knowledge of our Lord and Saviour Jesus Christ. To him be the glory both now and to the day of eternity. Amen* (2 Peter 3:18).

I sought the LORD, and he answered me and delivered me from all my fears (Psalm 34:4).

For further reading

All published by Day One Publications

- Robinson, Simon, *Help!—I'm caught up in a crisis*

- Edwards, Brian H., *Is It True? The resurrection of Jesus*

- Winter, Jim, *Depression: a rescue plan—a practical Christian response to depression*

- Gurney, Robert, *Six-Day Creation—Does it matter what you believe?*

- Bell, Philip, *Evolution and the Christian Faith: Theistic evolution in the light of Scripture*

- Fretwell, Thomas, *What does the Bible really say about...? Adam & Eve*

- Fretwell, Thomas, *Who Am I?—Human Identity and the Gospel in a Confusing World*

* Also look out for forthcoming titles in this 'Finding' series: the first three are: *Finding Life in Jesus, Finding Love in Jesus* and *Finding Peace in Jesus*. These concise helps in booklet form by Michael Austin follow this present title.